HOW CAN I GET SMARTER THAN THE TESTS I TAKE?

Check the questions below that you want answered by this book. You will find the answers in the chapters indicated. Also, short answers can be found on page 235.

Multiple Choice (Chapters 9 and 10)

_____ Why are so many tests made in this format?

_____ How do I choose between two answers when they both seem right?

_____ Which should I read first, the question or the answers?

_____ How do I handle choices like "All of the above" or "None of the above?"

True/False (Chapter 11)

_____ The statements always seem true to me. How do I know when a "true" answer is really false?

_____ Sometimes part of the question seems true and another part seems false. How do I know which to choose?

Matching Columns (Chapter 11)

_____ Why do instructors sometimes put more answers than questions on a matching column?

_____ When two answers are very similar, how do I know which one to choose?

IDs, Fill-ins, or Completions (Chapter 13)

_____ How much information is required? I never know how much to say.

_____ What do I do if I know the answer, but have forgotten the spelling?

_____ What do I do if I only remember part of an answer?

Essay Questions (Chapters 14, 15, and 16)

_____ Why are essay questions so popular?

_____ How do I make sure I don't run out of time when I write an essay answer?

_____ How do I figure out what to prepare before an essay test?

In General

_____ When—and how—should I guess on a test?

_____ How much time should I spend preparing for an exam?

_____ If I have to cram for a test, how do I do it?

_____ Should I study with other people?

W9-AUE-247

THE SECRETS OF TAKING ANY TEST

THE SECRETS OF TAKING ANY TEST

Second Edition

Judith N. Meyers

LEARNINGEXPRESS
NEW YORK

Copyright © 2000 LearningExpress, LLC.

All rights reserved under International and Pan-American Copyright Conventions.
Published in the United States by LearningExpress, LLC, New York.

Library of Congress Cataloging-in-Publication Data

Meyers, Judith N.
    The secrets of taking any test / Judith N. Meyers.—2nd ed.
      p. cm.
    Rev. ed. of: The secrets of taking any test in 20 minutes a day. © 1997.
    ISBN 1-57685-307-1 (pbk.)
    1. Test-taking skills. 2. Examinations—Study guides. 3. Study skills. I. Meyers, Judith N.
Secrets of taking any test in 20 minutes a day. II. Title.

LB3060.57 .M49 2000
371.26—dc21   00-032721

Printed in the United States of America
9 8 7 6 5 4 3 2
Second Edition

For Further Information
For information on LearningExpress, other LearningExpress products, or bulk sales,
please write to us at:
    LearningExpress®
    900 Broadway
    Suite 604
    New York, NY 10003

Or visit us at:
    www.learnatest.com

CONTENTS

INTRODUCTION
HOW TO USE THIS BOOK

So, you have to take a test. Is that a test—or a TEST!? No matter how old you are or how many tests you have taken, you probably feel a little grip of anxiety at the prospect of taking a test. You're not alone.

Most adults and even children and teens get a bit stressed when they have an exam coming up. But it often hits adults harder than younger people. Children and teenagers take tests routinely in school, so test taking is a familiar part of their lives. But if you've been out of school for a while, you're less accustomed to being judged in this manner. You may also have more pressure to succeed on a test if you are taking it to obtain or advance a career.

Adults are often more self-conscious than children in school. You probably judge yourself more harshly than any teacher would. It's easy for you to view a test not so much as merely a measure of some specific knowledge, but as a measure of yourself as an individual. So, naturally you're more likely to face tests with some measure of fear and anxiety.

This book is here to help. It has been written expressly for you, an adult learner, to help you overcome any test-taking anxiety you might feel and to help you become a savvy and effective test taker.

Think about this fact: As an adult, you have some real advantages over younger test takers. Here's why:

- You have a larger store of knowledge to draw upon.
- You have had life experiences where you've been tested in ways that have served to broaden your knowledge, helped you build your skills, and enriched your life.
- You have the maturity to be more organized in your planning and follow-through and more focused on your goals as you prepare for the tests you're going to take.

Don't forget about these assets as you read the test strategies in this book. Your strengths as an adult learner will serve you well.

WHAT TESTS ARE YOU GOING TO TAKE?

There are many kinds of tests that adults can take. Here are the most common:

- Standardized tests include the General Educational Development (GED) test, Scholastic Assessment Test (SAT), and American College Test (ACT). A passing grade on the GED gives you a high school equivalency diploma. The SAT and ACT are college entrance exams.
- Civil service tests are usually required if you're seeking a job with a local, state, or federal government agency.
- Classroom tests measure how well you've learned particular information and perhaps techniques and skills in courses, workshops, and the like.

Let's look at two general categories of tests.

STANDARDIZED TESTS

Some tests are standardized tests, where a person's performance is judged against the performance of hundreds or thousands of other people who have taken the same test. In other words, a standard of performance has been established and each test score is compared with that standard.

Some standardized tests measure *achievement*, or success in a particular area of study. Some familiar examples would be:

- Comprehensive Tests of Basic Skills (CTBS), which are exams children take in school
- General Educational Development (GED), which are exams taken for high school equivalency
- Tests of Adult Basic Education (TABE), which are exams taken for placement purposes in a college program

Other tests measure *aptitude*, or ability to master learning tasks. The most obvious example of such a test is the Scholastic Assessment Test (SAT).

Standardized tests are used for purposes of placement, class rank, promotional decisions, or entrance to training programs. Most of these tests follow a multiple-choice format. Answers are generally recorded on a bubble grid in pencil and are scored by computer (see Appendix A).

This format is favored by creators of standardized tests because it allows an objective standard of performance. This means that the creators of tests can't change the test to offer an advantage or a disadvantage to a particular group of test takers.

NON-STANDARDIZED TESTS

Non-standardized tests are those tests that seek to measure how well the learner performs on tasks that are related to a job or to the particular curriculum of a course. These include civil service tests and classroom tests.

Civil service tests usually measure how easily you can be trained to perform the job you're applying for. They don't test things you actually have to know to be a government clerical worker or a police officer, but they *do* test things like your reading and writing ability, your ability to solve problems, and specific abilities needed by the profession—good judgment for police officers, for instance, or your ability to alphabetize for a clerical job. Civil service tests are usually in multiple-choice format, though a few tests also have other formats such as essay writing.

Classroom tests are often made up of a number of question and answer formats that might include multiple-choice, true/false questions, matching columns, fill-ins, and essays. This kind of test is more flexible and allows greater leeway for instructors to emphasize particular topics and to assign grading weight where they think it is most appropriate. Some instructors even wait to assign point value to some areas of a test until the test has been given. This enables them to decide on what that value should be depending upon how well the largest numbers of students did on each section. The test also functions as an evaluation of the instructor's effectiveness. The instructor is, in fact, using the test to guide an assessment of how well he or she taught each section tested by the exam.

On the following page, think about your own experiences as a test taker and learn a little about the learner you are.

WHAT KIND OF TEST TAKER ARE YOU?

Check the sentences below that best describe your personal test-ability.

_____ **1.** I am always nervous about tests.

_____ **2.** I am nervous about tests only when I don't feel confident about my performance.

_____ **3.** Sometimes the more I study, the worse I do on exams.

_____ **4.** If I have the time to study, I score better.

_____ **5.** I do best on tests when I cram for them.

_____ **6.** When I take a test, I want to know the results immediately.

_____ **7.** When I take a test, I don't want to know the results immediately.

_____ **8.** When I get nervous on tests, I freeze up.

_____ **9.** I do better on essay questions than on short-answer questions.

_____ **10.** I do better on short-answer questions than on essay questions.

_____ **11.** I do better on tests when I study alone.

_____ **12.** I do better on tests when I study with a friend.

_____ **13.** I study better when I am in a quiet room.

_____ **14.** I study better when I can hear the radio or television.

_____ **15.** Sometimes I am surprised when I get a lower score than I expected.

_____ **16.** Sometimes I am graded unfairly.

_____ **17.** I sometimes get a better score on a test than I expected.

_____ **18.** I sometimes do better on standardized tests than on classroom tests.

_____ **19.** I sometimes do better on classroom tests than on standardized tests.

_____ **20.** I sometimes study the wrong things for a test.

My worst experience with a test was when

_____

because

_____

My best experience with a test was when

_____

because

_____

THE SECRETS OF
TAKING ANY TEST

CHAPTER | 1

What, when, and where: What tests do you need to take? And when and where will you take them? Read on to discover how you can find out.

FINDING OUT ABOUT THE TESTS YOU MUST TAKE

You can't prepare for a test until you know what test you'll be taking and when it will be given. If you are planning to go to college, you will probably need to take the ACT or SAT as part of your application process. If you're job hunting, you have to find out which tests are required for the job you want.

HIGH SCHOOL EQUIVALENCY TEST

If you don't have a high school diploma, you can take the General Educational Development (GED) exam to earn a similar certificate. This exam tests for knowledge in each of the key curriculum areas typically found in high schools. It's a very important test for anyone who expects to move on to higher education.

The GED is developed and administered by the Education Department in each state. Schedules of exam dates are available at public libraries or can be requested by writing to your state's Education Department in your state capital. GED tests are also administered at designated schools, agencies, and correctional institutions across the country.

You'll find preparation guides to the GED at libraries and in bookstores. GED preparation classes are offered at community colleges and high schools. Watch the paper for notices of continuing education courses and GED classes near you.

COLLEGE ENTRANCE TESTS

Most colleges require all applicants to submit their scores on one of these assessment tests—either the Scholastic Assessment Test (SAT I) or the American College Test (ACT). They may specify which one or give you your choice; it often depends upon where you live and what college you're applying to. Some colleges may also require one or more of the standardized subject tests known as the SAT II Subject Tests.

SAT

An SAT measures the general ability to do college work. SAT I measures verbal and mathematical reasoning abilities. SAT II Subject Tests (formerly known as the Achievement tests) measure mastery of secondary school subjects.

The SAT also includes a Student Descriptive Questionnaire that allows students to give information regarding their interests, educational objectives, and academic background.

Registration materials for the SAT I and SAT II can be obtained from a local high school, at the website, or by writing:

Educational Testing Service
1425 Lower Ferry Road
Trenton, NJ 08618
www.collegeboard.org
sat@ets.org

ACT

The ACT is another assessment test that's used to prove readiness for college work. It's required in place of the SAT by a number of colleges, particularly in the Midwest. The ACT includes tests in math, English, reading, and science reasoning. The scores on all four subjects are averaged together to give an ACT test score, which is more or less equivalent to the SAT score. ACT also has a battery of tests under the ASSET program by which colleges test students in reading, computation, algebra, and language skills for purposes of placement.

Applications for the ACT can be obtained from:
ACT, Inc.
Publications Dept.
2201 N. Dodge St.
P. O. Box 168
Iowa City, IA 52243
www.act.org

Fees for taking the SAT and ACT are waived for those who can provide proof that they are on public assistance.

TESTING TIMES

SAT and ACT exams are given several times a year. They are held on Saturdays, but those who cannot take Saturday exams for religious reasons may apply to be tested on the Sundays following the scheduled exams. The SAT I and the ACT exams are three hours each. SAT II exams each take one hour.

TOEFL

The Test of English as a Foreign Language test is required by some schools for students whose previous schooling was in another country. Information about TOEFL is available at

Box 899-R
Princeton, NJ 08541
(609) 771-7100
http://www.ets.org

TABE

TABE tests are for people who do not have a high school diploma or its equivalent because they have been educated in another country. If they wish to apply to U.S. schools, colleges, or other educational programs, they may take the TABE to prove competence in English, math, and reading skills. TABE tests are not typically used as admissions tests but are often used diagnostically, to place students in appropriate class levels in basic skills.

CIVIL SERVICE TESTS

The time and location of civil service tests are a little trickier to learn about since they're not usually posted in schools, where other exam information is readily available. It takes some persistence and networking to find out about when the exams for particular jobs are being given and to get the applications and other materials you need to take the exam. If you have Internet access, you can search under "Civil Service" to find test dates and applications.

TEST DATES

Civil service positions are usually posted at the offices of human resources or employment offices of city agencies or services. Information about the tests you need to take to be considered for such positions—with the police, fire, or sanitation departments and for jobs in skilled trades and clerical fields—are posted there as well. State, county, and city websites also list test dates and sometimes provide tests or job applications online.

If you live in a large city, you can often learn of the times and locations of civil service tests in magazines, newsletters, or pamphlets about civil service jobs in general or about the specific occupation in which you are interested. Newspapers like New York's *Chief-Leader,* a weekly civil service paper, contain notices of all upcoming examinations in every field that offers public employment.

In most communities, the public library is the best resource for information on upcoming tests. The library receives all materials related to examinations for public workers, so you can pick them up there. Ask at the front desk if you don't see them on display.

WHAT'S IN A CIVIL SERVICE TEST?
Basic Skills Tests

Many civil service exams test basic skills, such as reading comprehension, math competency, writing skills, judgment, and common sense. Most questions are multiple-choice. Questions are answered on a separate answer sheet that is scored by a computer.

Physical Fitness Tests

These tests are given to people applying for jobs as police officers, fire-fighters, and others whose jobs require physical strength. The tests measure height and weight (because there are minimum and maximum limits on size) and require the candidate to perform a number of physical tasks required by the job.

Special Skills Tests

There are some jobs that require specialized skills, such as typing or the use of specific computer software. Find out if you will need to take such a test for the position you're interested in.

CLASSROOM TESTS

In classroom tests, the arena is smaller and those giving the tests have more control over the test-taking process. Teachers and professors schedule tests and examinations at specific times during the year, either in the classroom or another specified room.

Classroom tests often contain a mixture of short-answer questions, multiple-choice, true/false, fill-ins, matching columns, and essays. This is because most instructors want to

1. Assess students' understanding of facts and information easily and quickly, which is best done with short-answer questions
2. Judge students' understanding and expression of larger concepts of class discussions and assignments, which is best shown in extended answers or essays

PLANNING FOR A CIVIL SERVICE OR STANDARDIZED TEST

Be sure you know about the test well in advance. Once you know when an exam is to be given, send for the application immediately so that you will have plenty of time to complete it and get it returned in time for the test.

After you get a copy of the application, follow these steps to complete the application process:

1. Make at least one copy of the application before you fill it out. Then you will have a spare if you make an error in filling it out, lose it, or spill coffee on it. Use the copy to practice on and then fill in and send the original form to the testing agency.

2. Read through the application or exam announcement for a description of what will be required for the job and what may be tested. Underline, circle, or highlight on your working copy of the application or announcement any additional tests you have to take along with the written test.

3. When you are applying to take an exam, keep a file with all the papers pertaining to that exam in a safe place. It is very easy in busy households to lose or mislay important papers. Make sure your exam materials don't go astray. Many exam packets contain a number of forms, such as admissions cards you'll need to get into the examining room and special instructions for completing the application. They are all important.

4. Be sure you know whether a personal check, money order, or certified check is required for test fees. Make a copy of the check and keep it with your other records.

5. When mailing applications and checks, it's a good idea to send them by registered mail, or mail them with a return receipt, so you get proof that the application was received and know when it was received. Keep such return receipts with your records.

If you have Internet Access, check to see if you can apply online and submit your application electronically.

PLANNING FOR A MAJOR CLASSROOM EXAM

You don't have to apply for classroom tests—they come automatically with the class! But you will want to find out exactly when they're scheduled so you'll be ready for them.

1. Check your course outline or syllabus carefully to note when the mid-term and final exams will be held.
2. Immediately write down the dates of major exams in your home and pocket calendars.
3. Make sure you have copies of all class notes, handouts, and texts that you need for the test.
4. Make a copy of your important notes and leave this second set at home in case you lose the originals.
5. Plan your schedule around the exam dates, and allow plenty of time for study and review.

TEST TAKING IN CYBERSPACE

In a world where virtually every life experience is going online—from childbirth to supermarket shopping—can virtual testing be far behind? There is little doubt that within the next few years more and more testing will be done via computer. Today many students already use computers to take tests by e-mail or on interactive websites. Classroom tests can be put on disks for students to take at home or in school computer labs. In addition, standardized test makers are making it possible to take *computer adaptive tests* (CATs) at centers located around the country. At present, relatively few tests are given in the CAT format. The GRE (Graduate Record Examination), nursing, and architectural boards use the CAT. Test takers should be familiar with how these tests are given, however, as the trend for the future is clearly in this direction.

WHAT IS A CAT?

A CAT literally adapts itself to the individual test taker. In these tests, the student's answers on the first few questions determine the level of difficulty of the questions that will follow. Thus the test taker is given only those questions he or she is likely to answer correctly. The level of the questions is weighted, however, so that answers on harder questions are worth more points.

How Are CATs Administered?

Students register for an appointment at a testing center. They are each assigned to a testing station, which contains a computer and a mouse. Test takers are given a brief tutorial on the workings of the computer and the testing program. They then log on to the test and begin working. Directions on the screen take the student through the various sections of the exam. Students select an answer and then click to confirm the answer before it is recorded. When the exam is over, the student can choose to have the scores calculated by the computer immediately or choose to have the scores mailed to home some weeks later.

What Are the Advantages of CATs?

For people who use computers all the time, CATs provide a comfortable method for test taking. The individualized nature of the test means that each test taker has a unique version of the test, based on his or her ability to perform specific operations. This virtually eliminates any problem of cheating. The other advantage for some people is the instant feedback possibility in a CAT. You don't have to wait several weeks to learn test scores. For good or ill, you know how well you did on the test immediately. In addition, the many sites—usually at commercial learning centers—make it possible to offer more dates to take a test.

What Are the Disadvantages of CATs?

The CAT is software driven. You must rely on the machine to fine-tune the questions you are given. If you are nervous or inexperienced with computers, test taking by computer may not be to your advantage. In addition, on a CAT you can only work with one screen at a time. You cannot scroll back to previous questions to change an answer. This may be frustrating to students who are accustomed to being able to return to previous questions for further consideration.

General Hints for Taking Any Test on a Computer

1. Feel absolutely comfortable with the machine.

If you only work on one program at work and perhaps use your home computer mostly for word processing or recipe keeping, you should think about spending some time learning how to use other computer programs, websites, and other Internet resources. Most public libraries have computer access and staff who can help you to navigate past the basics on an unfamiliar machine. It would help to practice until you feel truly confident that you can find your way around several programs.

2. Manage your time wisely.

Time management is important for all test taking, but there are specific situations that are part of taking a standardized, *timed* test on the computer. Take all the time you need studying the tutorial you are given at the beginning of the test. Most tests have a Help function available throughout the test, but usually the time spent being helped is time away from the test. In addition, some tests have a time crawl on top or below the text, alerting the student as to how much time they have left. If this is distracting to you and makes you more nervous, you should simply hide the crawl and rely on your watch to measure your time on each section.

3. Take charge of your own test.

When you take a standardized test that is computer adapted, the computer has a great deal of power. It is constantly monitoring your performance because its selection of questions is determined by your choice of answers. It doesn't allow you to return to questions for further thought. It penalizes you for random guessing because a wild guess will determine the level of the next question, but it doesn't allow you to skip questions for the same reason. Therefore, it is critical that each test taker be very assertive in the way he or she approaches the test. Here are some guidelines for taking the CAT:

Guess right. Since making educated guesses is so important in a test that penalizes poorly chosen answers, be sure your guesses result from a savvy elimination of choices that are likely to be wrong. We talk about this in detail in Chapter 21. On a computer test, where you don't have the ability to physically cross out your eliminated answers, you can do the same thing on the scrap paper you are given at the test site. Quickly jot down 1-2-3-4 or a-b-c-d on your paper, and cross out the options as you eliminate them. This will narrow your choices and allow you to concentrate on picking the answer most likely to be correct.

Front load your time. Since the computer will base its selection of questions on your responses to the first few questions in each section, be sure you spend the longest time on those questions. Don't linger over later questions, because you need to be sure to answer all the questions in the section. Make your educated guesses and then move on. But give a bit more time to the earlier, pace-setting questions that are more important to the level at which you will be working and, therefore, to your overall score.

Be comfortable in the setting. Just as in any other test-taking situation, give yourself the advantage of wearing comfortable, layered clothing. Have tissues, gum, and cough drops handy if they are allowed. If you are relying on your watch to keep the time, be sure you have a new battery in the watch or that it keeps accurate time. Follow the other suggestions included in this book about rest, exercise, and mental preparation for the exam.

Later chapters will go into more detail on planning for a test and managing your study time.

On the following page, fill in the information needed for the kind of test you expect to be taking. Check your answers on the sample answer page that follows.

In Short

You need to be prepared to take any test. First, find out what test you need to take: the GED, SAT, ACT, TABE, civil service, CAT, or classroom test. Then, obtain the information you need as soon as possible so you can begin to prepare for the test.

TEST PLANNER

Exams I must take this year

_____

Exams for this job or course are currently scheduled for

_____

Filing deadline

_____

The location of this test is

_____

I will find information about this exam by checking the

_____

People I know who have taken this course or test

_____

Three things I need to know about this test are

_____

_____

_____

TEST PLANNER
(Completed sample)

Exams I must take this year
Firefighter's Exam

Exams for this job or course are currently scheduled for
November 10th

Filing deadline
October 1st

The location of this test is
Stuyvesant Branch Library

I will find information about this exam by checking the
Chief-Leader newspaper and the Public library

People I know who have taken this course or test
Joe Martin—friend

Three things I need to know about this test are
Do I have to take a physical?
How much math is on the test?
Is there a good test preparation book available?

CHAPTER | 2

You need a plan, and this chapter will tell you all you need to know to put together a study plan that will help you prepare for the test or tests you have to take.

MAKING A STUDY PLAN

Preparing for a test is most effective if you have a system that keeps you focused on a very specific goal. And your goal, of course, is to get the very best score possible. As in most things in life, the more you plan to succeed, the more often you will succeed. And remember, your true goal is not just to get by on a test; it's to do well on the test.

This chapter guides you step-by-step through the process of setting up a study plan for a standardized, civil service, or classroom test.

STEP 1: SET A TIME FRAME
STANDARDIZED TESTS

Most standardized tests are only given a few times a year, so you'll need to get those dates and plan around them. You should allow anywhere from *two to six months* to prepare for a test like the GED, ACT, or SAT.

CIVIL SERVICE TESTS

Civil service tests for the positions of firefighter, law enforcement officer, sanitation worker, clerk, or skilled trades worker require approximately *three to four months* to prepare fully for the test.

CLASSROOM TESTS

For a major classroom test, such as a mid-term or a final, you need to determine your preparation time according to several factors:

- **How much does the test "count"?** If a major test counts for half or a quarter of the final grade, you will want to allow about two weeks ahead of the test date to prepare. Some finals or mid-terms count the same as other exams. If that's the case, you will need to review a little each day for at least a week.
- **How many other tests are you taking at the same time?** If you are taking several tests in a short period of time, you need to make a schedule that will assign a reasonable amount of time to each of the tests, quizzes, and papers that are due. (More about this later!)
- **What is the test worth to you at this moment?** In other words, how well are you doing in the course right now? What does this test mean to this course? If you are achieving an "A" in the course, you may want to spend less time because you have already demonstrated progress in the class and have a good grasp of the subject. If your earlier test marks in a particular class are low, you'll want to plan on a longer preparation time. You'll need to spend extra time studying the material.

STEP 2: GET THE CORRECT INFORMATION
STANDARDIZED TESTS

Check filing dates for the standardized test you need to take. Find out if you will be taking subject tests on the same day. Check your testing kit. Read the directions and suggestions for success that come with the papers you receive with the sample test.

Civil Service Tests

Check filing dates for the civil service test you want to take. Check your testing kit. Preview the skills that will be tested. Note whether there are special skills tests included, such as physical fitness, typing, or computer literacy tests.

Classroom Tests

Check your calendar to see whether you have other tests at or near the same time. Ask the instructor about the format of the test: Is it going to be short-answer or essay? Will you do it in class or take it home? Find out how long the test will be and what specifically will be covered. Assess how much the test means to your final grade.

Step 3: Get All Your Materials
Standardized and Civil Service Tests

Find some review books or other materials you might need to prepare for the test. If you're proficient on the Internet, you can find test-preparation help for most standardized tests using a search engine such as Yahoo! or Lycos. Find out if there are any test preparation courses available to you in your community.

Classroom Tests

Look over your notes to be sure they are clear. If they are not, try comparing notes with another student. Finish any reading or other assignments you may have missed. Check to make sure that you have all handouts.

Step 4: Stay on Your Plan

Treat yourself to an afternoon walk, a candy bar, a long phone chat with a friend—anything that will reward you for maintaining a good study schedule. It isn't easy, and you should pat yourself on the back when you can stick to your routine for some period of time.

SAMPLE STUDY PLANS

Because each type of test is different, each should have its own study plan. Here are some examples to get you started thinking about what you will need for your study plan.

STANDARDIZED TESTS

This schedule is for an important and comprehensive test that requires lots of preparation time, like the SAT or ACT.

Four to Six Months Before the Test

1. Request all materials needed for the test.
2. Buy a large desk or wall calendar and enter the test dates for your test.
3. Browse the bookstores or libraries for review books or computer CDs that contain sample tests. Buy or borrow only one or two that seem appropriate. Too many books can be expensive and overwhelming. Note what other resources are available to you through the Internet or from print material. (See Additional Resources at the end of this book.)

> **Whose Books Are They?**
> Don't be tempted to borrow textbooks or review books from another student to save money. When test time nears, guess who will be the one with the book? The one who paid for it—of course!

4. Analyze the format of the test. Is it all multiple-choice? How many questions are in each section? How long does the test take?
5. Take two sample tests from a review book. Check your scores on the tests. See how you performed on each part of the test. The strategies you are learning in this book should help you complete even these commercial practice tests more successfully.
6. Write down the two areas in which you scored the lowest on both of the two practice tests: math, spelling, reading comprehension, and so on.
7. Do two more sub-tests for each of the areas in which you scored lowest.
8. Based on these early practice sessions, decide if you need help. For example, do you need to work with a tutor or perhaps take a review class in math or English?

Eight Weeks Before the Test

1. Set aside one hour a day to review the test areas you want to improve. Do just the parts of each test you want to work on—as many as you can do in an hour—for four days a week. Do a complete review test three times a week.

2. Keep a chart or graph of your scores on the review tests (see p. 242). Take note of your progress. Are your scores going up? Are they uneven?

3. Organize a study group with others who will be taking the test. There are some drawbacks to this (see Chapter 3), but study groups are helpful to some test takers.

Four to Six Weeks Before the Test

1. Confirm the date of the test.

2. Confirm that your application has been received and that you have been sent all the necessary materials.

3. Make sure you know where the test will be held and how you will get to the test site.

4. Continue to review for half an hour to an hour five days a week. Notice that, contrary to expectations, you are spending fewer hours a week in preparation. If you have been reviewing regularly for a couple of months, the reviews should take you less time since you're so accustomed to the questions. This is the most important part of preparing for tests. The more familiar you are with the test, the better you will perform under testing conditions.

5. Meet with your study group. Encourage each other; a positive attitude is a big help.

One Week Before the Test

1. Take two more review tests. See how your scores compare with the tests you took at the beginning. Don't become anxious if you do less well than you think you should at this point. The reality is that you *do* know more than when you started, and it will show when you actually take the test.

2. Concentrate on being well-rested and relaxed about the test.

3. Make sure you have all necessary items—pencils, watch, calculator, gum—and have arranged for plenty of time to get to the test site.

CIVIL SERVICE TESTS

Again, timing is very important. Some civil service tests are given at regularly appointed times during the year, and you can choose which time you want to take the test based on your own time limits with work, school, and family obligations. More often, however, a test is scheduled for a particular day, sometimes with several months' notice and sometimes with only a few weeks' notice.

If you have the time, you should be generous and allow yourself four to six months, just as you would if you were taking one of the standardized tests described above—then you can use that study plan. However, you might find that you have less time than you'd like to prepare because the test is scheduled with little prior notice. If your time is shorter, here is a sample study plan that can guide you. It's designed for approximately two months of fairly concentrated study.

Eight Weeks Before the Test

1. Confirm test dates and registration procedures for the test.
2. Get at least one review book that contains sample tests.
3. Take the first sample test. Score it. Note the areas in which your scores were low.
4. If your scores were very low in one or more major areas—math or English usage, for example—decide if you need to take a class or get individual help to boost your scores.
5. Set aside two half-hour periods a day. If there are exercises in the review books, do them. If you need other practice materials, look in the bookstore or library or on the Internet for additional sources of help.

Six Weeks Before the Test

1. Take a second practice test. Compare your scores. Note your areas of weakness on this test.
2. Continue to review weak areas for at least 30–45 minutes a day.
3. Use the study strategies you will learn in the following chapters.

Four Weeks Before the Test

1. Take a third practice test. Again, compare your scores and note areas of weakness.
2. Determine if you would benefit by working in a study group. If so, organize one.
3. Continue practice exercises.

Two Weeks Before the Test

1. Take a fourth practice test. Compare your score with the first three practice tests you took.
2. Continue to do practice exercises at least four times a week.
3. Confirm the date and location of the test. Make sure you know how to get to the test site, and make travel arrangements to get there in plenty of time.

One Week Before the Test

1. Look back over the sample tests and exercises that you've done.
2. Meet with your study group, if you have one. Encourage each other.
3. Remind yourself of how much you have learned.
4. Study for two days during the week, and review only those items that still seem difficult.
5. Get plenty of rest and exercise. Avoid stress and anxiety as much as possible.

CLASSROOM FINAL EXAMS

Naturally, classroom tests differ according to the subject matter, the purpose of the test, the number of students being tested, and the preference of the instructor. Your preparation will depend on how well you're doing in the class, the level of interest or importance to you of the subject matter, and how much time you have to devote to this subject.

Large sections or classes, especially in math or science, may take tests on separate answer sheets that are electronically scored. Other tests in the humanities and social sciences may require extended answers and essay questions that will be graded by the instructors or their teaching assistants.

The following is a sample study plan for a final exam in a college course.

Two Weeks Before the Test

1. Review your grade status in all your classes.
2. Review your grade status in this class.
3. Review the syllabus (course outline) to find out what percentage of your final grade depends on this test. Ask the instructor whether the test will cover the entire semester's work or just the material dealt with since the last test or the mid-term.
4. Ask about the format of the test. Will it be short answer, essay, or a combination?
5. If you missed any classes, photocopy a classmate's notes for those classes. Collect any handouts distributed by the instructor.

Ten Days Before the Test

1. Review all textbook reading. Read margin notes and the text that is highlighted or underlined in the assigned chapters. Review all class notes. Borrow a set of notes from a classmate, and make a copy of them.
2. Arrange for at least one study session with another student. Compare notes with that person and discuss possible areas of emphasis on the test.
3. If you are uncertain about any aspect of the course and if there is a lot riding on this test, this would be a good time to make an appointment with the instructor to clarify any parts of the material you don't understand. Be sure that you take your class notes and a list of at least three specific questions to the meeting.

One Week Before the Test

1. Create study notes from text and class notes. Write information to be memorized on cards. Begin intensive study of factual material: dates, names, facts, and terminology. Use study strategies from Chapter 4.
2. Write out possible extended answers to essay questions.
3. Outline answers to help organize information in your mind.

Two Days Before the Test

1. Review notes and handouts.
2. Re-read text notes.
3. Reduce notes to a handful of cards or pages that can be used for quick last-minute review as you work on other courses.

One Day Before the Test

1. Review notes and assigned reading material one more time.
2. Eat well and exercise. Go to bed early.
3. Face the day with confidence!

THE TEST PREPARATION BOOK MARKET

There is an enormous market in test preparation or review books these days. The study plans we have outlined in this book assume that you will spend at least some preparation time working through or consulting commercial review materials. When you go to the store to purchase your review books, however, you may find that the huge selection is overwhelming. In addition, since the cost of a review book is generally somewhere between fifteen and twenty five dollars, you may want to be sure that the books you purchase are going to meet your needs. Here are some tips for selecting review materials.

- **First think about you as a learner. Ask yourself these questions:**
  How much *experience* do you have with taking important tests?
  How *important* is this test to you?
  How much *time* do you have to use a review book? *Where* will you be using the book?
  What *kind of text* appeals to you? (Do you like a chatty, informal style? Do you like a more serious, no-nonsense approach?)
  How much can you *spend* on review materials?

- **Now think about the book choices you have. Ask yourself these questions:**
  What is does the book look like? What is its format, size, and general content? Most review books are paperbacks that are intended to be consumable. That is, the publishers expect the books to be written in and used up. Some are 8-1/2-by-11-inch books, small enough to

fit into a bookbag or briefcase. Others may be 9-by-12 inches and three to four inches thick. The larger books may be difficult to keep with you outside of your main study area.

Some books are quite visually appealing. They have cartoons, lots of wide margins and text and print that is shaded to highlight important information. Some are chock full of strategies and tips for dealing with test questions. They may have appealing icons that appear regularly in the text to alert the reader to important strategies or testing tips. Other books have denser text and depend more on the test taker to discover the methods he or she needs to deal with different testing tasks. Some books have relatively little to say about test taking strategies, but provide a great deal of practice material.

Ask others who have taken the test for recommendations on the books they used to prepare for the test. Don't ask to borrow someone else's test prep book. The whole idea here is to practice putting in your own answers. You don't want to confuse yourself by looking at how someone else answered the questions.

What is the author's writing style?

If you are going to spend several weeks working your way through a review book, you should select the writing style that fits your approach to the test. For example, some review text writers employ a breezy, conversational, often humorous style. These writers invite the reader to prepare for the test almost with a sense of personal competition with the test makers. This kind of approach is often appealing to young people or inexperienced test takers who like to feel that they are outsmarting the test writers. These books may also be helpful to those who are especially anxious about testing and find that the informal tone of makes them feel more relaxed and confident. Other test takers prefer a more business-like approach that allows the test taker to practice without much guidance from the author. While at the bookstore or library, skim through a few pages of a prospective test book to sample the writing style. Choose the "voice" that speaks to you.

Does the book offer extra features that might be helpful?

No doubt because of the keen competition in the test preparation market, many publishers of review materials include add-ons with their books as an incentive to purchase the material. Such extras include computer software bundled with the book, discounts for computer-based practice materials, guides to college applications, and test preparation timelines. Check out the extras. If they don't apply to you, then the book may not be a good choice to meet your needs.

A WARNING ABOUT REVIEW BOOKS

Classroom test takers, beware of using the test prep book as a substitute for fuller study. Students taking courses in certain subject areas may benefit from using a review book in math, biology, or grammar to enhance their general knowledge of the subject. But be careful of using one of the "Notes" books, however, instead of, for example, reading *Moby Dick* or *Madame Bovary*. Most instructors are very much aware of the kinds of questions included in those books and may be very suspicious of essays that sound as though they were copied or adapted from those materials. In addition, each teacher will have his or her own take on the themes, characters, and plot lines of the novels they teach and will want to see those ideas reflected in the work submitted by their students. Use the "Notes" books to reinforce, not to replace assigned reading in class.

AT THE BOOKSTORE

The best selection of test preparation materials is usually found in the large chain bookstores. The benefit of those stores is that they allow you to spend as much time as you like browsing through the books. Take your time and be selective about the materials you choose. Here is a systematic way of sampling the offerings.

1. **Pick out two or three books** that look interesting, and find a corner where you won't be in the way of other browsers.

2. **Skim the whole book first.** Note the format, print size, and numbers of practice tests included in the book.

3. **Read the introduction to the book.** Get a feel for the guiding philosophy of the writers or publishers.

4. **Check the publishing date** to make sure you have the most recent

edition of the book.

5. Read through the directions and through the first few pages of at least two of the review tests. Make sure you can follow the directions easily and that there are enough practice tests to help you, but not so many that you feel discouraged about getting through the book.

6. Think about your own specific needs for review. If you need to review particular content—math skills, grammar or history, for example—you may want to buy a smaller, general review book and also purchase one or more of the skill guides that are available.

7. Think about how you intend to use the book. Will you be using it as your primary review source or as a reference book for extra practice around other review resources on the Internet or in a test prep class? No need to buy the larger, more comprehensive books for spot review.

The hardest part about making a plan is actually starting the plan. On the next page you have an opportunity to outline a plan for your test or tests by thinking through what you want to know about the test and how you can get prepared to do your best. Compare your answers with those on the completed sample study plan that follows.

In Short

You need to create a study plan to schedule your time leading up to a test. After you establish how much time you have to prepare for the test, gather all your test materials and review books to help establish your specific plan. Since your plan will differ depending on what type of test you are taking, you need to create a separate plan for each type of test.

YOUR OWN STUDY PLAN

In the space below, write in a schedule for the two months prior to taking a standardized, civil service, or classroom test.

The test I need to take is

_____

It will be held on

_____

The test site is located at

_____

Three questions I have about the test are

_____

_____

_____

I plan to study for this test as follows:
Two months before the test

_____

One month before the test

_____

Two weeks before the test

_____

One week before the test

_____

Two days before the test

_____

The day before the test

_____

YOUR OWN STUDY PLAN
(Completed sample)

In the space below, see a completed sample of a Study Plan for the two months prior to taking a classroom test.

The test I need to take is
Biology 101 final

It will be held on
Dec. 15

The test site is located at
Murrie Hall

Three questions I have about the test are
Will my lab grades count?
Will it be multiple-choice?
How much does the test count?

I plan to study for this test as follows:
Two months before the test
Make sure I have the handouts and notes since mid-term.

One month before the test
Keep up with reading assignments. Do all labs and look at finals schedule.

Two weeks before the test
Check my grades in this class against other classes.

One week before the test
Create study notes, study with group. Outline chapters, make maps.

Two days before the test
Memorize phyla, other basic facts. Create final study notes.

The day before the test
Review notes and go to bed by 11.

CHAPTER | 3

Now you'll find out how to make the plan you've created work for you: where to study, who to study with, and how to make the most of your time.

CARRYING OUT YOUR STUDY PLAN

Don't rely on luck and savvy. With an important test, it's just too risky. Staying casual about your exam, playing the procrastination game, and only dabbling with a study plan could very well mean sabotaging your chances of success.

Taking a test is a lot like taking a trip. The better it's planned, the more pleasant the journey. While you may say that you like to be spontaneous and let the spirit move you in taking off on a trip, you might find that you wind up with no place to stay, you've brought the wrong clothes, and you're trying to do too much in too short a time.

The same thing can happen with a test. You may find that you've given too much priority to studying minor topics, that you haven't managed your test preparation schedule well, or that you lose your momentum part-way through the test itself.

The best study plan in the world, however, is only as good as how well it's completed. Here are some suggestions for carrying out your study plan to its successful conclusion.

LOCATION, LOCATION, LOCATION

Find a quiet spot, have a good reading light, and turn the radio off.

FIND QUIET PLACES

For many adult test takers, the only quiet spot they know in their busy lives is the bathroom. Many adults don't even have a bedroom corner that isn't shared with someone else. Your quiet spot may be in a different place at different times of the day. For example, it could be the kitchen table early in the morning before breakfast, your workplace area when everyone else is at lunch, a corner of the sofa late at night. If that's the case, make sure your study material is portable. Keep a folder or bag that contains your notes, practice tests, pencils, and other supplies. Then you can carry your study materials with you throughout the day and study in whatever quiet spot presents itself.

If quiet study areas are non-existent in your home or work environment, you may need to find a place elsewhere. The public library is the most obvious choice. Some test takers find it helpful to assign themselves *study hours* at the library in the same way that they schedule dentist appointments, class hours, household tasks, or other necessary uses of daily or weekly time. Studying away from home or job also minimizes the distractions of other people and other demands when you are preparing for a test.

LIGHTS

Libraries also provide good reading lights. For some people this may seem like a trivial matter, but the eye strain that can come from working for long periods in poor light can be very tiring—a cause of fatigue you can't afford when you're studying hard. At home, the bedside lamp, the semi-darkness of a room dominated by the television, or the bright sunlight of the back porch will be of little help to tired eyes.

Many of the review books that contain sample standardized tests have small print, often on newsprint-style paper. You need a good light just to see what you are working on!

ABOUT THAT RADIO

Certainly, if you have a radio playing in the room where you are studying, it is not going to be a quiet place. But many people swear that they can't concentrate in a room that's too quiet. They need the background noise of a radio or television to screen out the smaller noises generated by the life going on around them.

This is the reasoning of many teenagers. Given the level of constant auditory input of most young people, it does seem that they are lost without constant background music in their lives. For adults who have so little time to prepare for exams because of other demands on their time, and who need to get as much mileage out of each precious hour of study as possible, the radio or television is too distracting.

If you do enjoy some sound in your study environment that's not just the beating of your own heart, however, be selective about the times you study with the radio on. The radio may be a good companion when you're reviewing old notes, writing study cards, or otherwise gathering information for study. However, silence is golden when you're trying to memorize, taking a practice test, or thinking through a math example.

Remember that there won't be any radio or television in the background when you're actually taking the test. It's probably a good idea to get used to working on test material in the same general atmosphere of quiet in which you'll take the test.

PARTNERS IN PREPARATION

Once you have a study plan in place, you might also want to consider the roles of other people (significant or otherwise) who are involved with your preparation for the test.

Preparing for a test, whether it's just a short period of time for a classroom test, or months for a civil service or standardized test, often means emotional and psychological wear and tear on you and those close to you. Your parent, spouse, or sweetheart may resent the time that your study plan takes from activities you usually do together. They may not be as supportive and sensitive as you'd like them to be.

They may not realize that you have to forego the weekly trip to Grandma's for Sunday dinner because you have to study. And if by chance you're the grandma, you may have to let your family know that you won't be back in the kitchen until the test is over!

Keep Them Involved and Aware

Here are some ways to minimize hurt feelings and resentments that come up during exam crunch time:

- Let your family and friends know what you need to do. Share your study plan with them.
- If your study plan covers several weeks or months, sit down with the people in your life, and work the plan around everyone's important needs. Look at the calendar together, and plan your study or reviews so that they don't interfere with significant events such as holidays, important family gatherings, or work obligations.
- Keep a calendar with the details of your study plan where everyone can see it. Then anyone who needs to can look on the calendar to see when you will be busy. They might be less likely to put extra pressure on you at those times.
- Ask for help. Even young children can help someone to study. Family and friends can quiz you on facts you must memorize, talk through difficult ideas, and take over some of your chores to give you time to study. Don't be afraid to ask for help, and then let people help you when you need it most.
- Show appreciation for their efforts to support and encourage you. Remember, your test may test the patience of everyone involved.

STUDY GROUPS

There's not necessarily any reason to study alone. If you're taking a test, then others are too. Studying with one or more people can give you the motivation, support, and fresh perspective you need at such times.

Choose your study group members with care. If you are lucky enough to know other test takers well, then you can pick people whom you respect. You can meet with people you already know from your class or within your community, or you can post notices on a school bulletin board to reach others whom you don't know but who may be seeking this kind of support for a big test.

You may want to start your study group informally. Get together with a few people who are taking the same test. Talk with them to get a feel for how motivated they are and how they want to study together. If you don't feel comfortable with some or all of the group, you haven't made a commitment or wasted your time. If the group seems to be compatible, you can arrange for other meetings.

PROS AND CONS OF A STUDY GROUP

There are several advantages to working in a study group:

- You have the benefit of the notes, insights, and ideas of other people.
- Listening to the ideas of other people helps to clarify information for you.
- Study group members can offer support and encouragement to each other.

There are also some drawbacks to working in a study group:

- Sometimes when people get together they spend more time socializing than studying.
- Some group members may be competitive and not be willing to share information or resources with others.
- Some group members may tend to slack off and not take test preparation seriously, which can mean that they wind up not doing their share of group work.

ORGANIZING A STUDY GROUP

How you choose people and structure the group can make all the difference in its ultimate success. One question you may consider at the outset is whether to study with friends or with strangers. There are benefits with and drawbacks to each choice. Some people feel more comfortable with friends or people they know well. They feel less competitive, perhaps, and are more willing to ask questions or share information with people with whom they have some prior association. On the other hand, groups that are too chummy may be groups that spend too much time socializing. This fact is why some people prefer a more businesslike or arms-length relationship with their "study buddies." They feel more comfortable with other students they do not know outside the classroom because they waste less time on personal conversation and spend more time on reviewing important material. Of course, groups made up of strangers lack the supportive feeling of a closer group, but they may also be more efficient by making better use of limited time.

Regardless of whether your group is comprised of friends or strangers, here are some tips to help your group to succeed:

- Keep it small; three to six people is best. Larger groups are less easy to manage.
- Appoint one person to be the contact person to arrange sessions.
- Have your study group meet in as neutral a place as possible. An ideal location for a study group in is a classroom after scheduled classes. Many college libraries also have study rooms that will accommodate a few people who want to work together without disturbing others with their talk.
- Start each group session by creating an agenda or list of topics the group will discuss. Always decide at the beginning of each session how long you will work.
- Ask everyone to come to the meeting prepared with notes, questions, and patience.

SETTING YOUR SIGHTS

An important part of implementing any study plan is organizing that plan so it accomplishes a specific goal. In your case, it is probably to get a top grade. That overall goal, however, is best accomplished by setting and meeting a series of shorter goals that all lead to a high test score.

The study plan, as you recall, has four basic steps:

1. Set a time frame.
2. Make sure you have the correct information about the test.
3. Gather all your classroom and test preparation materials together.
4. Stay on your plan and reward yourself for it.

Think of each one of these steps as a goal that will get you closer and finally take you to your ultimate goal. Then think of the time you need to accomplish these goals.

TIMING TRICKS

All the plans in the world won't help, of course, if you don't find time to actually study what you need to pass the test. It's like choosing recipes, shopping, and assembling the ingredients for a fancy dinner and then not leaving enough time to prepare and eat it. You have to find the time to put your plan into action.

MAKING YOUR PLAN FIT YOU

Here are some strategies for testing your plan against what you know about your personal time patterns and commitments:

- **Figure out what time you have available to study in a typical week.** Write down what you do on one typical work day and one typical weekend day.
- **Notice what hours seem to be free for study.** Are most of those hours in the evenings? In the daytime? How *many* hours are available for study? Is your study time in blocks? (Wednesday afternoons and Saturday mornings, for example.) Or is your study time in bits and pieces during the week? (An hour each morning and half an hour late in the afternoon before the bus comes.)
- **Determine your own patterns of rest and fatigue.** Are you a morning person who can get up an hour early and study before breakfast? Are you a night owl who can work after everyone else is asleep? Are you accustomed to exercising regularly? Does exercise tire or energize you?

Answering these questions will help you to choose the times that are best for you to study for your test. Once you've answered the questions, consider how your time frame fits the study plan you've devised by completing the Weekly Timetable at the end of this chapter.

STICKING TO YOUR PLAN

Now that you have a plan that will work, here are some strategies for sticking to it:

- **Write down your study schedule.** Post a copy where it will remind you of the times you need to study.
- **Don't abandon your study plan if you get off track for a few days.** It's easy to become discouraged when outside events, work obliga-

tions, family responsibilities, or personal problems keep you from your studies during the time you have scheduled for studying. Just pick up where you left off. Try to add a little time to two or three study sessions rather than trying to make up for lost study time by cramming or by skipping important material.

- **Adjust your study plan to meet changing needs.** For example, if you find that you need to do more practice tests than you had planned to do, take more time to do them. If you find that you are doing well on specific sections of the practice tests and less well on others, take more time on those sections that need your attention.

Remember that the purpose of the study plan is to organize your study time, not to dictate how to run your life or to make you feel guilty.

Now it's time to create your own Weekly Timetable on the next page that incorporates all your responsibilities, including study time. If you're not sure what to include, take a look at the completed sample at the end of this chapter.

IN SHORT

You can successfully carry out your study plan by finding a quiet location to study in, using adequate reading light, turning off the radio and television, asking your family and friends for help, and organizing a study group. Setting your study goals and writing down your study schedule will help you to master the material on your test.

WEEKLY TIMETABLE

On the timetable for a week below, cross out any hours when you are occupied with work, family, recreation, meals, and any activities you do on a regular basis—team sports, community work, volunteer work, and so on. See what hours you have "free" to study.

	Sunday	Monday	Tuesday	Wednesday	Thursday	Friday	Saturday
6:00							
7:00							
8:00							
9:00							
10:00							
11:00							
12:00							
1:00							
2:00							
3:00							
4:00							
5:00							
6:00							
7:00							
8:00							
9:00							
10:00							
11:00							
12:00							

WEEKLY TIMETABLE

(Completed sample)

	Sunday	Monday	Tuesday	Wednesday	Thursday	Friday	Saturday
6:00							
7:00							
8:00							
9:00							
10:00							
11:00							
12:00	←	L U N C H			→		ERRANDS
1:00							
2:00							
3:00							
4:00							
5:00		DINNER					
6:00							
7:00							RECREATION
8:00				MEETING			
9:00			BOWLING				
10:00							
11:00							
12:00							

CHAPTER | 4

Read on to discover how
to adapt your study
strategies to the ways you
learn best—and to pick
up some smart new
techniques to help you
prepare for your test.

LEARNING STRATEGIES

How successful you are at studying has less to do with how much time you put in to it than with *how* you do it. That's because some ways of studying are much more effective than others, and some environments are much more conducive to studying than others. Another reason is that not everyone retains information in the same way.

LEARNING STYLES

Think for a minute about what you know about how you learn. You've lived long enough to have a good feel for how you learn what you need to learn. For example, if you need directions to a new restaurant would you:

- Ask to see a map showing how to get there?
- Ask someone to tell you how to get there?
- Copy someone's written directions?

Most people learn in a variety of ways: seeing, touching, hearing, and experiencing the world around them. Many people find, however, that they naturally tend to get information better from one learning source than others. The source that works best for you is called your dominant *learning modality*.

There are three basic learning modalities: the visual, the auditory, and the kinesthetic (also known as *tactile*).

- **Visual learners** understand and retain information best when they can *see* the map, the picture, the text, the word, or the math example.
- **Auditory learners** learn best when they can *hear* the directions, the poem, the math theorem, or the spelling of a word.
- **Kinesthetic learners** need to *write* the directions, *draw* the diagram, or *copy* down the phone number.

VISUAL LEARNERS

If you are a visual learner, you learn best by seeing. Pay special attention to illustrations and graphic material when you study. Color code your notes with colorful inks or highlighters. Learn to map or diagram information (see later in this chapter).

AUDITORY LEARNERS

If you are an auditory learner, you learn best by listening. Read material aloud to yourself, or talk about what you are learning with a study partner or a study group. Hearing the information will help you to remember it. Some people like to tape-record notes and play them back on the tape player. If you commute to work or school by car or listen to a personal tape player, you can gain extra preparation time by playing the notes to yourself on tape.

KINESTHETIC LEARNERS

If you are a kinesthetic learner, you learn best by doing. Interact a lot with your print material by underlining and making margin notes in your textbooks and handouts. Rewrite your notes onto index cards. Recopying material helps you to remember it.

IMMERSION LEARNERS

Adults have a special advantage as learners because their lives and life experiences can assist the learning process. Make the most of your life experience to add to your personal data base of language and information. Read widely in newspapers and magazines. If you have a career focus or are preparing for a specific kind of job, subscribe to the journals, newsletters and newspapers in that field or occupation. Keep a clipping file of articles related to the career you have in mind. Watch television programs that explore important current events, documentaries, and works adapted from literature. Carry a small notebook in which you jot down interesting words you hear at work on the radio or on TV. When the time comes to take a test, all of that information you have stored contributes to what you can bring to the writing of an essay or making the correct selection on a multiple choice question. This fact is particularly important when it comes to answering judgment questions (more about this in Chapter 10). If you have a good sense of issues that are important to the business you want to be in, you will be better able to judge the kind of answer the test maker thinks is important.

HOW TO STUDY MOST EFFECTIVELY

If studying efficiently and effectively is second nature to you, you're a rare bird indeed. Most people have to work at it. Here are some helpful study methods.

MAKING AN X-RAY

After collecting all the materials you need to review or prepare for the test, the first step for studying any subject is to reduce a large body of information into smaller, more manageable units. One approach to studying this way is to *x-ray* text information, handout material, and class notes.

Think about an x-ray. It is a picture of the bare bones of a body. The important information in print material is often surrounded by lots of extra words and ideas. If you can highlight just the important information, or at least the information you need for your test, you can help yourself narrow your focus so you can study more effectively. There are several ways to make x-ray pictures of print material. They include annotating, outlining, and mapping.

Annotate with Restraint
Annotation should be thoughtful and selective. Underlining everything in the text prevents the "skeleton" of the text from being seen.

Annotating

Annotation means that you underline or highlight important information that appears in print material. It also involves responding to the material by engaging the writer in "conversation" by means of margin notes. Margin notes are phrases or sentences in the margins of print material that summarize the content of those passages.

- Annotations pull out main ideas from the surrounding text and make them more visible and accessible.
- Margin notes leave footprints to follow in a review of the text.

Here is an example of a passage from Chapter 3 that has been annotated and underlined.

LOCATION, LOCATION, LOCATION

Find a quiet spot, have a good reading light, and turn the radio off.

FIND QUIET PLACES

Different quiet places at different times

For many adult test takers, the only quiet spot they know in their busy lives is the bathroom. Many adults don't even have a bedroom corner that isn't shared with someone else. Your quiet spot may be in a different place at different times of the day. For example, it could be the kitchen table early in the morning before breakfast, your workplace area when everyone else is at lunch, or a corner of the sofa late at night. If that's the case, make sure your study material is portable. Keep a folder or bag that contains your notes, practice tests, pencils, and other supplies. Then you can carry your study material with you throughout the day and study in whatever quiet spot presents itself.

Bag for study materials

If quiet study areas are non-existent in your home or work environment, you may need to find a space elsewhere. The public library is the most obvious choice. Some test takers find it helpful to assign themselves study hours at the library in the same way that they schedule dentist appointments, class hours, household tasks, or other necessary uses of daily or weekly time. Studying away from home or job also minimizes the distractions of other people and other demands when you are preparing for a test.

Library!

LIGHTS

Libraries also provide good reading lights. For some people this may seem like a trivial matter, but the eye strain that can come from working for long periods in poor light can be very tiring—a cause of fatigue you can't afford when you're studying hard. At home, the bedside lamp, the semi-darkness of a room dominated by the television, or the bright sunlight of the back porch will be of little help to tired eyes.

Need good light

Outlining

You are probably familiar with the basic format of the traditional outline:

    I. Main idea 1
        A. Major detail
        B. Major detail
            1. Minor detail
            2. Minor detail
    II. Main idea 2
        A. Major detail
        B. Major detail

You may have used an outline to help you organize a writing assignment. Many writers outline their work before they begin to write.

When you outline print material, you're doing just the reverse: You're looking for the outline of the idea that has been buried in the text. When you are taking out the important information for a test, then you are looking for the x-ray of what the author wanted you to know.

Here's how you could outline the main ideas in Chapter 3 of this book, "Carrying Out Your Study Plan":

    I. Places to study
      A. Home
      B. Library
        1. Light
        2. Quiet
    II. Who to study with
      A. Family
      B. Study group
        1. Advantages
        2. Disadvantages

Mapping

Mapping is a more visual kind of outline. Instead of a making a linear outline of the main ideas of a text, when you map, you make a diagram of the main points in the text that you want to remember. Again, using the text from Chapter 3, the next page shows the same information in a map.

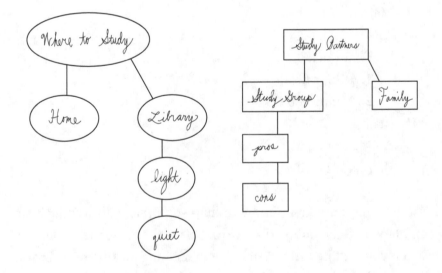

The point of all three of these strategies is that they allow you to pull out just the important information that you need to prepare for the test.

MAKE STUDY NOTES

The next step after you have pulled out all the key ideas is to make notes from which you will study.

Study notes are the notes that you will use for the intensive and ongoing study you'll do over a period of time before the test. They're the specific items that you targeted as important to know for the test and the tools by which you will learn to understand that information and, in many cases, commit it to memory.

What kind of information do you put on study notes?

- The main ideas you underlined or highlighted in the text
- The main ideas and important details you outlined or mapped from the text
- Specific terms, words, dates, formulas, names, facts, or procedures that you need to memorize.

How Do You Make Study Notes?

Some people like to write study notes in the back pages of their notebooks or on paper folded lengthwise so that it can be tucked between the pages of a text or review book. This format is good to use for notes that can be written as questions and answers, cause and effect, or definition and examples.

20th century	women writers
Toni Morrison	Sula
Joyce Carol Oates	Them
Ayn Rand	The Fountainhead
Virginia Woolf	To the Lighthouse
Betty Friedan	The Feminine Mystique
Alice Walker	The Color Purple

Using Index Cards

Most study notes, especially those that contain material to be memorized, should be written on index cards.

There are a few advantages to making notes on index cards:

- The information on each card is visually separated from other information. This allows you to concentrate on just that one item, separate from the surrounding text. You remember the look of a vocabulary word or a math equation more clearly when it is set off by itself.
- Cards are small and portable. They can be carried in a purse or a pocket and pulled out at odd times during the day for review, without the bulk and inconvenience of a book or notebook.
- Study cards are the means by which you can work on the necessary task of memorizing.

MAKING MEMORIZING EASIER

There are many ways to take the drudgery out of memorizing information.

Take Short Bites of Time

Most people memorize information best when they study in small periods over a long period of time. This is called *distributed practice.*

Memorizing facts from index cards that can be pulled out for a few ten-minute sessions each day will yield better results than sitting down with a textbook for an hour straight. Index card notes can be pulled out in odd moments: the ten minutes you are sitting in the car waiting for your child at Little League, the eight minutes you spend waiting for your roommate to get ready to go to dinner, or a quiet fifteen minutes on the bus.

You'll find that these short but regular practices will greatly aid your recall of lots of information. It's a sneaky and painless way to add more study time to your schedule.

Break It Up

When you have a list to memorize, break the list into groups of seven or any other odd number. People seem to remember best when they divide long lists into shorter ones—and, for some reason, shorter ones that have an odd number of items in them! So instead of trying to memorize ten vocabulary or spelling words, split your list into smaller lists of seven and three, or five and five, to help you remember them.

Make Associations

You memorize best when you can attach meaning to what you are learning. In order to do this, you need to make associations with the material by *translating* the information into a practical example you can imagine in your own life.

Create Visual Aids

Give yourself visual assistance in memorizing. If there's a tricky combination of letters in a word you need to spell, for example, circle or underline it in red or highlight it in the text. Your eye will recall what the word looks like.

Do It Out Loud

Give yourself auditory assistance in memorizing. Many people learn best if they hear the information. Sit by yourself in a quiet room, and say aloud what you need to learn. Give your notes to someone else, and let that person ask you questions to be answered aloud.

Use Mnemonics

Mnemonics, or memory tricks, are things that help you remember what you need to know.

The most common type of mnemonic is the *acronym* (a word created from the first letters in a series of words). One acronym you may already know is HOMES, for the names of the Great Lakes (Huron, Ontario, Michigan, Erie, and Superior). ROY G BIV reminds people of the colors in the spectrum (Red, Orange, Yellow, Green, Blue, Indigo, and Violet).

You can make a mnemonic out of anything. In a psychology course, for example, you might memorize the stages in death and dying by the nonsense word DABDA (denial, anger, bargaining, depression, acceptance.) Another kind of mnemonic is a silly sentence made out of words that each begin with the letter or letters that start each item in a series. You may remember *Please Excuse My Dear Aunt Sally* as a device for remembering the order of operations in math (parentheses, exponents, multiply, divide, add, and subtract).

Sleep on It

No one has yet figured out a way that people can just put the book under the pillow and wake up the next morning with its contents stashed neatly in their brains. But it is true that when you study right before sleep and don't allow any interference—such as conversation, radio, television, or music—to come between study and sleep, there is better recall of material. This is especially true if you review first thing after waking as well. A rested and relaxed brain seems to hang on to information better than a tired and stressed-out brain.

Sleep in Your Bed—Don't Study in It

You might think it makes sense, after a long day, to take a shower and get ready for bed so that you can read the chapter, memorize the vocabulary, and take the review test in comfort. Unfortunately, this is the quickest way to send yourself straight to sleep. You are out of study mode the minute you hit that mattress.

It certainly makes sense to find a place to study that is comfortable. And sometimes a shower can wake you up and make you feel refreshed. But your bed is probably too comfortable to be useful.

If you want to make reading in bed of some use to test preparation, don't try to seriously study in bed. Rather, use that time to read newspapers, magazines, and books that will make you well-informed on a variety of subjects. If you have chosen a major in school or are interested in a particular job category such as law enforcement or firefighting, keep a file of clippings about that field. Even tests that are geared to skills, rather than facts, will often ask you about information that you may have learned through your reading. The more general knowledge you have, the more you bring to the testing room.

On the following page there are exercises on annotating, mnemonics, mapping, and study card writing. After you complete the exercises, check out how you did by looking at the suggested answers that follow.

IN SHORT

You can learn to study more effectively for any test by creating an x-ray of the material you need to know. If you annotate, outline, and map study notes, the material will be easier for you to review. Studying in short bites of time, breaking up long lists of memory work into shorter ones, making associations, and creating mnemonics will help you learn the test material efficiently and effectively.

TRY OUT SOME LEARNING STRATEGIES

Annotation

Below is a passage from this text to underline and annotate. Make margin summaries of the key points in each paragraph. Then make a mnemonic based on your margin notes.

Take Short Bites of Time

Most people memorize information best when they study in small periods over a long period of time. This is called *distributed practice*.

Memorizing facts from index cards that can be pulled out for a few ten-minute sessions each day will yield better results than sitting down with a textbook for an hour straight. Index card notes can be pulled out in odd moments: the ten minutes you are sitting in the car waiting for your child at Little League, the eight minutes you spend waiting for your roommate to get ready to go to dinner, or a quiet fifteen minutes on the bus.

You'll find that these short but regular practices will greatly aid your recall of lots of information. It's a sneaky and painless way to add more study time to your schedule.

Break It Up

When you have a list to memorize, break the list into groups of seven or any other odd number. People seem to remember best when they divide long lists into shorter ones—and, for some reason, shorter ones that have an odd number of items in them! So instead of trying to memorize ten vocabulary or spelling words, split your list into smaller lists of seven and three, or five and five, to help you remember them.

Make Associations

You memorize best when you can attach meaning to what you are learning. In order to do this, you need to make associations with the material by *translating* the information into a practical example you can imagine in your own life.

Create Visual Aids

Give yourself visual assistance in memorizing. If there's a tricky combination of letters in a word you need to spell, for example, circle or underline it in red or highlight it in the text. Your eye will recall what the word looks like.

Do It Out Loud

Give yourself auditory assistance in memorizing. Many people learn best if they hear the information. Sit by yourself in a quiet room, and say aloud what you need to learn. Give your notes to someone else, and let that person ask you questions to be answered aloud. Tape record your notes and play them back to yourself at home or in the car.

Use Mnemonics

Mnemonics, or memory tricks, are things that help you remember what you need to know.

The most common type of mnemonic is the *acronym* (a word created from the first letters in a series of words). One acronym you may already know is HOMES, for the names of the Great Lakes (Huron, Ontario, Michigan, Erie and Superior). ROY G BIV reminds people of the colors in the spectrum (Red, Orange, Yellow, Green, Blue, Indigo, and Violet).

Note Cards

Make note cards with definitions for each kind of learning modality:

- Visual
- Auditory
- Kinesthetic

Mapping

Below is an outline of the learning strategies covered in this chapter. Using the same information, make a map, or diagram, of the same material.

I. How to x-ray a text
   A. Annotating
   B. Outlining
   C. Mapping
II. How to make study notes
   A. Notebook pages
   B. Index cards
      1. Reasons for using index cards
III. Memory methods

TRY OUT SOME LEARNING STRATEGIES
(Completed sample)

Annotation

Take Short Bites of Time

Most people memorize information best when they <u>study in small periods over a long period of time. This is called *distributed practice.*</u>

Memorizing facts from index cards that can be pulled out for a few ten-minute sessions each day will yield better results than sitting down with a textbook for an hour straight. Index card notes can be pulled out in odd moments: the ten minutes you are sitting in the car waiting for your child at Little League, the eight minutes you spend waiting for your roommate to get ready to go to dinner, or a quiet fifteen minutes on the bus.

You'll find that these short but regular practices will greatly aid your recall of lots of information. It's a sneaky and painless way to add more study time to your schedule.

Distributed practice

Break It Up

When you have a list to memorize, <u>break the list into groups of seven or any other odd number.</u> People seem to remember best when they divide long lists into shorter ones—and, for some reason, shorter ones that have an odd number of items in them! So instead of trying to memorize ten vocabulary or spelling words, split your list into smaller lists of seven and three, or five and five, to help you remember them.

Divide lists

Make Associations

You memorize best when you can attach meaning to what you are learning. In order to do this, you need to make associations with the material by <u>*translating* the information into a practical example you can imagine in your own life.</u>

Translate

Create Visual Aids

<u>Give yourself visual assistance in memorizing.</u> If there's a tricky combination of letters in a word you need to spell, for example, circle or underline it in red or highlight it in the text. Your eye will

Visual Aid

recall what the word looks like.

Do It Out Loud

Auditory

Give yourself auditory assistance in memorizing. Many people learn best if they hear the information. Sit by yourself in a quiet room, and say aloud what you need to learn. Give your notes to someone else, and let that person ask you questions to be answered aloud. Tape record your notes and play them back to yourself at home or in the car.

Use Mnemonics

Mnemonics, or memory tricks, are things that help you remember what you need to know.

Acronym

The most common type of mnemonic is the acronym (a word created from the first letters in a series of words). One acronym you may already know is HOMES, for the names of the Great Lakes (Huron, Ontario, Michigan, Erie and Superior). ROY G BIV reminds people of the colors in the spectrum (Red, Orange, Yellow, Green, Blue, Indigo, and Violet).

Sample Mnemonic: DADVAT

Note Cards

Here are samples of how your note cards might look:

Visual modality— learning by seeing	*Auditory modality— learning by listening*	*Kinesthetic modality— learning by touching or moving*

Mapping

Here is an example of how your map or diagram might look:

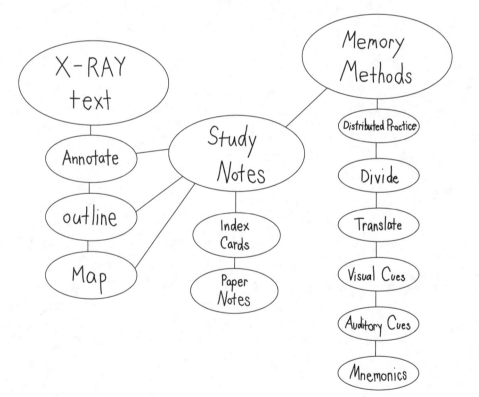

CHAPTER | 5

Do you ever get all tense—or worse—before an exam? There's relief for you in this chapter. You'll learn constructive strategies for preventing and treating cases of test anxiety.

COPING WITH TEST ANXIETY

Test anxiety is like the common cold. Most people suffer from it periodically. It won't kill you, but it can make life miserable for days. Like a cold, test anxiety (TA for short—let's give it a nickname, so it's more comfortable to talk about.) can vary in severity. Sometimes it's no more than a little sniffle of dread about an upcoming exam. Sometimes it's a full-blown attack of what feels like imminent death. There are people who seem to be more vulnerable to TA in general and suffer badly from it. Others are better able to cope with the symptoms and get over it quickly. The point is, some degree of TA is inevitable for most, so until there is a cure, you need to find ways to deal with the affliction.

SYMPTOMS OF TEST ANXIETY

A mild case of TA may only feel like a few butterflies in your stomach as you head toward your testing room and a little shaking of the hands as the test is given out. Both symptoms subside as soon as you become absorbed in taking the test.

Actually, a little TA is beneficial. That slight adrenaline rush is energizing and stimulates concentration and attention to the task of test taking. Not to worry.

If you're stricken with a more severe bout of TA, you probably have persistent feelings of dread or fear, changes in your patterns of eating and sleeping, and occasional unusual mood swings. Some people fear that they will "freeze" while they are taking the test and be unable to perform successfully, even if they know the answers.

Such heavy-duty TA is not a good thing. Take a big dose of this chapter to cure yourself of it!

HELP FOR SEVERE TEST ANXIETY

Dramatic, crippling TA is fairly uncommon, but when it strikes, it may actually make it impossible for some people to take tests that could be important to them. People who suffer from this condition are quite literally paralyzed with fear. They become overwhelmed by it, and the consequences are severe mental and physical distress that could include vomiting, fainting, weeping spells, and depression.

If you suffer stress of this kind, the kind that doesn't diminish with simple, practical management techniques, you should seek counseling before preparing yourself for an important exam like a civil service test or the GED.

CAUSES OF TEST ANXIETY

Why do people suffer from TA in the first place? Well, TA grows out of the risks of doing poorly on a test. Depending on what kind of test you have to take, those risks might include many different things.

Many concerns about testing are real, such as:

- Failing an expensive or important course
- Losing a job
- Failing to qualify for a job
- Not getting into the course, college, or program you want

In the midst of a TA attack, you may manage to make matters worse by adding less concrete but equally scary risks such as

- Disappointing yourself (*I always knew I was stupid!*)
- Disappointing others (*What will my wife/dad/child/teacher think of me?*)
- Facing an uncertain future (*What happens to me now?*)
- Repeating the failure (*I can't take this all over again!*)

PREVENTING TEST ANXIETY

As with most unhealthy conditions, the best cure for TA is prevention. The more you can ward off an attack of TA, the better you will do on your test. Here are some preventive measures:

- **Keep a well-organized routine in your life.** Try to minimize the small problems that clutter up your mental landscape. Keep in mind that most minor problems are resolved without major fanfare.
- **Reduce as much general stress as you can.** A stressed-out life is a fertile field for test anxiety.
- **See the good, smart, resourceful person in the mirror every day.** Any time you're ready to beat yourself up about something, remind yourself of something good about yourself. (*I don't believe I made that stupid comment. On the other hand, I'm glad I wrote that note to Jane. She really seemed to be touched by it.*)
- **Stay healthy.** This is one of the most important ways you can keep from being overtaken by worries and anxieties of any kind. Diet and exercise help create a sense of well-being that prevents the more severe forms of TA.

TREATING TEST ANXIETY

Inevitably, despite all the preventive maintenance you do, you're bound to develop at least some of the signs of TA. Here are some suggestions for managing it when it strikes.

STEP #1: CONFRONT YOUR FEARS

Standing up to fear is the same as standing up to a bully who would rob you of your self-esteem and confidence. Look it in the face and refuse to be intimidated.

Put Your Fears on Paper

Think about the real and imagined risks of failure on your test. *Write them down.* They will seem much smaller on the page than they do in your head. Do this especially if you get into the habit of waking up in the middle of the night with your brain racing with imagined horrors of failure. Get up. Turn on the light. Take out a piece of paper. In two columns write down the fear (now called the *problem*) and what to do about it (now called the *solution*). Here's an example:

Problem	Solution
I have to go to the family reunion this weekend. How will I find the time to stick to my study plan? What if I fall behind?	I'll take my index cards with me and I'll find some short periods of time to review some vocabulary. I'll get my wife to quiz me in the car.

Think About the Worst That Could Happen

Another mind game to play is *worst case scenario.* Ask yourself what the very worst outcome of failure would be. Then ask yourself, "So what?" Will the world come to an end? Will my mother or spouse stop loving me? Am I less of a person than I was before the test?

Of course not. Perspective is very important to performance. It is necessary, of course, to be serious about success. But it is not necessary to lose sight of other important aspects of your life.

STEP #2: BE OVERLY PREPARED

Probably the best prescription for success when you take any test (and certainly the best medicine for TA) is being so prepared that the risks of failure almost disappear. This remedy goes beyond the mere limits of systematic study, however. It means to *over-learn* your material.

Over-learning is just what the word implies: learning the material so well that your answers to questions are practically automatic. An obvious example of over-learning for most people is the multiplication tables. They repeated them so often while in school that they can retrieve them without conscious thought.

Over-learning is accomplished in several ways. It isn't just a matter of adding to the number of hours you spend studying for your test. It means learning in a specifically active, self-directed way. To over-learn, use all of your senses:

- *Look* at the information.
- *Write* the information.
- *Talk* the information through with someone else so you can absorb it and relate to it.
- *Listen* to yourself and someone else talk about it.

Become so familiar with the material that you don't even have to hear all of the question before you say the answer.

STEP #3: EXCUSE YOURSELF FROM EXCUSES

When people do poorly at something or are afraid they might do poorly, they tend to find excuses for their failures. Some of these excuses seem to make a lot of sense and do contain some elements of truth:

- "I didn't have enough time to study because of work, family, and community demands on my time."
- "I got sick before the test and couldn't study."
- "I couldn't understand the teacher, the textbook, or the test."
- "I'm just no good at those tests anyway. No matter how hard I try, I just can't get a good grade, so why bother?"

The problem with excuses is that they don't take away the test anxiety. They make it worse by adding another layer of guilt and nerves to the process. Excuses take away your power over your own actions. You are reduced to being a victim of time/health/bad tests/bad teachers/bad luck. Accept the reality of possible sickness, heavy schedules, or difficult courses.

Another remedy for TA, then, is to take control over your own behavior in response to challenges. Take personal responsibility for your study, and you'll feel the grip of anxiety lessen.

STEP #4: VISUALIZE SUCCESS

One of the ways you can take charge of your behavior in the face of test anxiety, possibly worsened by excuses and guilt, is to literally imagine your way to success. This is done by visualizing.

The term *visualizing* may be familiar to you because it is used often these days by sports psychologists and trainers working with athletes and others who suffer from performance anxiety. These people are trained to envision the success toward which they are driven. A runner makes a mental picture of the goal line. The gymnast imagines the announcer reeling off a row of perfect scores following a competition: *ten, ten, ten, ten.*

You, too, can envision yourself seeing an *A* posted on the bulletin board next to your name, or the celebration at home after you pass that critical test for the police or fire department. Keeping your mental eye on the prize that the test brings you is an effective—and pleasant—antidote to the stress of test anxiety.

STEP #5: BLOCK YOUR ESCAPES AND TAKE DOWN YOUR DEFENSES

Another way you can empower yourself to defeat TA is to overcome two common tendencies to escape the discomfort posed by the fear of failure. One escape route is through *procrastination.* The other is by means of *defense mechanisms.*

Procrastinating—deliberately or unconsciously delaying study until it's too late to succeed—is a good way to sabotage your own best efforts in preparing for a test. The more you procrastinate, the more guilt you feel. The guiltier you feel, the more you worry. The more you worry, the worse the outcome on the test.

Block that temptation to delay by making and sticking to your study plan. Put your review book or study notes out where you can't avoid them. Write notes to yourself and leave them on your mirror or pillow, in your lunch bag, or over the visor in your car. You can't run from yourself forever!

Another way you may try to defend yourself is by holding back from a real push to success because of a fear that your best isn't good enough. You feel better if you can say, "Well, if I'd had the time/health/ support/encouragement, I could have passed." It's discouraging to say, "I did my absolute best, and I still failed."

The problem is that you don't need the additional burden of discouragement on top of a bout with TA. Remember that you're an adult, and you've been tested before. Give it your best shot. After all, a good, solid try is still your best defense against failure.

IN SHORT

A slight case of test anxiety (TA) may help you concentrate on the test. However, a more severe case of TA can sabotage your success, so you should actively prevent or eliminate it. TA is caused by fear and can be prevented by staying organized, reducing other stress, staying healthy, and being positive. You can eliminate TA by confronting your fears, over-learning the test material, giving up excuses, visualizing success, and overcoming procrastination.

MANAGING YOUR TEST ANXIETY

Before you take a major classroom, civil service, or standardized test that makes you anxious, write down answers to the following questions.

I want to do well on this test because

_____

_____

What is the worst thing that could happen if I fail this test?

_____

_____

(See? Your fears already look less scary when you see them written down.)

How would I handle it if I did do poorly on the test? What would I do?

_____

_____

Some things I could do to keep myself from suffering from test anxiety are

_____

_____

When I see myself doing well on this test, I picture

_____

_____

MANAGING YOUR TEST ANXIETY
(Completed sample)

I want to do well on this test because
I need my GED to get a better job.

What is the worst thing that could happen if I fail this test?
If I don't get my GED, then I won't get a better job, and I'll have to stay in this dumb job forever.
(See? Your fears already look less scary when you see them written down.)

How would I handle it if I did do poorly on the test? What would I do?
I would study harder and take the test again.

Some things I could do to keep myself from suffering from test anxiety are
work out, study one hour per day, and practice deep breathing.

When I see myself doing well on this test, I picture
handing in the test at the end with a big smile and hugging my girlfriend

CHAPTER | 6

This chapter's all about test fitness—getting yourself mentally and physically prepared for the test ahead. You need rest, a healthy diet, and plenty of exercise in order to be in tiptop shape for your exam.

GETTING MIND AND BODY IN SHAPE

Examiners are accustomed to facing rows of bleary-eyed, unshaven, unkempt test takers who look like they just staggered in from a car crash. Serious students are seen as the ones with the shaking hands and ashen faces that speak of days of coffee and cigarette diets and nights spent in intense preparation. There are certainly those who appear to have a kind of perverse pride in how they have suffered in preparation for the exam. They boast of the all-nighters they have pulled, how they've lived on coffee and take-out meals for a week, how they took three days off from work to cram for the exam and are now exhausted. However, this does not have to be!

As you have seen, good mental preparation will do wonders to alleviate test anxiety and help you to study efficiently. Your mind will be better prepared to work for you if it is housed in a body that is well-tuned and maintained.

You count on good health to permit you to live the busy, often hectic life you lead. If you let yourself become vulnerable to sickness, you are adding to the likelihood that valuable time will be lost as you cope with illness and its inevitable feelings of weakness and fatigue.

SLEEP

Doctors and other health care professionals have long asserted that adults need 8 hours of sleep to function well in their daily lives. You are reminded by mattress salespeople that *one-third of our lives* (8 out of 24 hours) is spent in bed, presumably asleep. You might manage just fine on less than 8 hours of sleep on a regular basis, or at those times when your schedule just doesn't allow you to sleep that long. But not getting what is for you a good night's sleep will take its toll eventually—and you don't want that to happen during a test.

When Do You Need Sleep?

Think about what times of the day or night you are most tired. After work? Early evening? Late evening? When you first wake up? Try to sleep as much as you can during the times that your body is asking the loudest for rest. To struggle through a couple of hours of study after dinner or late at night when you are too tired is going to yield poorer results than taking a nap after work or after dinner and studying later with a rested mind. If you feel fresher in the morning, go to bed earlier and get up when the house is quiet so you can study before breakfast. If sick kids, job worries, or your own poor health keep you up for a couple of nights, make a concentrated effort to catch up on your sleep so that the accumulated fatigue doesn't slow you down.

What Happens If You Don't Sleep?

Realize the consequences of not sleeping. Studies show that human beings can maintain performance on tasks even when denied needed sleep. They will likely show other signs of disturbances, however, such as irritability, short-term memory problems, and headaches. In addition, less sleep means every activity requires more effort, so the fatigue compounds itself. Therefore, though you may be able to keep going despite less sleep, the spill-over of ill temper, physical discomfort, and weariness into the other parts of your life may be too costly. Understanding those costs may help you to be more cautious about putting yourself into a position of having no choice but to stay up late and cram.

WHEN SLEEP WON'T COME

Sometimes your concern with sleep is not how much sleep you can get or save, but how to get some at all. Often when you are anxious about a big test or have gotten overtired at work or with study, you find it difficult to fall asleep and then lie awake and worry about not sleeping. Here are some ways of coping with insomnia:

- **Study.** Many times just lying down with a book will put you instantly to sleep. Keep your dullest text by the bed and turn to it when sleep won't come.
- **Exercise.** A physically tired body will demand sleep over an exhausted, wound-up mind.
- **Relax.** Use relaxation techniques such as hot baths, warm milk (there is stuff in there that makes you sleepy), or a massage to unkink tight muscles.

FOOD

Maintaining a healthy diet is one of the hardest things to do during a test preparation period. You are probably studying for tests on top of a life that is already filled with time-consuming responsibilities. You automatically get rid of any activity you can that won't significantly impact on things if it's not done.

Food shopping, meal preparation, and cleaning up are easily substituted activities, especially today when fast-food is so accessible and, well, fast. Therefore, you would rather run to a fast-food restaurant with the family than spend time in the kitchen making a salad, or order a pizza that will be delivered in the time you complete a review test or memorize math theorems. It sounds good on the surface, but it's a bad habit to get into.

DIET PITFALLS

One reason to avoid the fast-food trap is that prepared food is loaded with salt. Even youthful cardiovascular systems are ill-served by high sodium levels. Salty foods invite thirst-quenching doses of soda, many of which are full of caffeine.

Pre-test nervousness, boredom, and procrastination cause many people to want to snack while they study. You find all kinds of excuses to get up from your studying and get something to eat. Nervous snacking can easily be substituted for meals (*I'm not hungry, I'll just pick*) or, worse yet, is in addition to regular meals and can contribute to unhealthy weight gain.

The easiest and most convenient snacks seem to be chips, crackers, and cookies—all unhealthy food, despite some packages' claims of low sodium and low cholesterol. These snacks often contain high fat levels, and they are normally eaten when you're sitting still and not exercising. That is a recipe for poor nutrition right when your body needs all the health it can get. Here are a few hints on how to avoid diet pitfalls:

- Buy bags of veggie sticks or fruit for study snacking. Don't allow soda or chips in the house.
- Limit the times you give in and order out. Let that pizza or Chinese take-out be the reward to yourself for achieving a study goal. Don't let it be your way of life during exam preparation. That kind of habit has a way of sticking around long after the test is done.

DRINK

While on the subject of food, let's also take aim at drinks as well. Apart from the above-mentioned caffeine-loaded soda, you should limit coffee and tea intake as well. Here, of course, is the Catch 22: You need to use caffeine to stay awake to study, but you need to limit the caffeine so it doesn't keep you awake or make you too jittery. (Isn't this fun?)

If you are a heavy or dependent coffee drinker, choose the times you must have a caffeine jolt—after dinner and just before study, for example. Other times during the day, drink decaffeinated soda or coffee. Your body may not even feel the difference. Some coffee drinking is more habitual than needful. The point is not to drink excessive amounts of coffee during test preparation periods. You may end up with coffee nerves that you don't need on top of test anxiety.

The other beverage issue is, of course, alcohol. Like studying in bed, having a beer or two while you study might seem like a good idea at the time. It's relaxing and makes you feel good when you're tired and stressed out. Like studying in bed, however, alcohol and books are a bad mix.

If you enjoy a beer or glass of wine, save it for your personal reward list for study well done. Don't ever think that a drink will help you study or overcome an attack of test anxiety. Alcohol will do just the opposite. It may put you to sleep when you should be studying, and it is a depressant that robs you of some of the coping mechanisms you need to manage test anxiety.

TOBACCO AND OTHER DRUGS

Again as with alcohol, dependence on cigarettes or other substances can only interrupt the body from working smoothly with the brain. If you smoke, this is probably not going to be the time to quit. But try to limit your smoking as much as possible prior to a test because of nicotine's effect on heart rate, blood pressure, and respiration. Dependence on tobacco also works against you because it can be a distractor if you have to worry about getting a cigarette on top of the worry of the exam.

People who would use other, stronger drugs while under the pressure of test taking are taking large chances on developing problems that are much bigger than any exam. If you take any prescription drugs regularly, you should never add any large amounts of food, coffee, tobacco, or alcohol without checking with your doctor to rule out side effects from mixing substances.

EXERCISE

Now that you've been denied all the joys of hamburgers, cigarettes, brews, and coffee, the test should seem like the least of your problems! There is another way that you can help prepare physically for an exam without having to deny yourself any fun. In fact, the very best thing you can do to prepare yourself physically for a test is to enjoy the fun of regular exercise. Even people who do not normally exercise very much will find that building in time for mild regular exercise pays off, not only in good test results, but also in habits of well-being that go beyond the test date. An exercise program will help in several ways. It will

- Keep your heart and lungs strong
- Help maintain your weight
- Stretch muscles that stiffen while inactive
- Stimulate appetite
- Improve sleep patterns
- Break up prolonged periods of study
- Provide an outlet for tension brought on by anxiety

Exercise for the test taker should be *mild* and *consistent*. The weeks and months leading up to a big exam should not be the time to undertake some dramatic and time-consuming sport or activity in the name of training for the test. Some people can easily transfer their energies to the wrong side: "I would love to do a review test for my exam, but I have to do my daily hour workout at the gym across town."

The general rule of thumb is that to keep healthy in the ways that are helpful to test preparation, you need to exercise at least three times a week, and each session should include 20 minutes of aerobic movement that will get your heart and lungs working at an increased rate. There are any number of activities that will produce these results without taking more than half an hour. They include

- Swimming laps
- Riding a bike, inside or outside
- Walking at a faster rate than a stroll
- Jogging
- In-line skating

In addition, playing an individual or team sport several times a month will help to keep your body fit. Playing games can also give you an opportunity to get away from the pressure of the exam and to enjoy some social interaction you may be missing while immersed in your study plan.

On page 74, you have the opportunity to think about your own needs for sleep, food, drink, and exercise. See how well you can plan a healthy time period before your exam. Then take a look at the sample completed form that follows this chapter.

A WORD ABOUT CHEATING: MENTAL FITNESS ALSO INCLUDES HONESTY

The very subject of test taking begs the question of cheating. It seems likely that for as long as people have been taking tests, some people have tried to give themselves an extra advantage by cheating. Cheating takes any number of forms—getting a copy of the exam ahead of time, for example, or sneaking notes with formulas or other information into the exam room. Some cheaters look at or are given answers by a fellow student. Some students attempt to recycle a friend's or family member's term paper or book report to fulfill class requirements. New technology has opened up a new set of opportunities to cheat. Recent news accounts report that there is a cottage industry in term papers available over the Internet. In addition, as we look around at the world at large, we see numerous examples of apparently successful people cheating on taxes, in their marriages, and in business. It is possible, then, to find reasons for cheating on exams.

ACCEPTABLE REASONS TO CHEAT ON AN EXAM:

There are no acceptable reasons to cheat on an exam.

UNACCEPTABLE REASONS TO CHEAT ON AN EXAM:

"I don't have time to study. I have no choice but to take a 'short cut.'"

"The course is unimportant." (*see also* boring, hard, not in my major)

"Everybody else cheats. If I don't cheat, *I* am at an unfair disadvantage."

Let's look at these reasons:

Blaming time constraints: It usually takes more time to prepare to cheat than it does to prepare for the test. Time and "negative" energy are spent plotting access to the hall with cheat notes, devising strategies for hiding "cheat sheets" up your sleeve or written on your hand, locating someone who has a copy of the test or persuading someone to give you the answers.

Blaming the course: It happens, of course, that we always like some courses better than others. And we respond to some teachers better than others. Some courses are more important to us or our careers than others. It is short sighted, however, to assume that because we didn't choose to take a course that it has no relevance to our education. Also, we aren't given an opportunity in the workplace to choose only those tasks that we enjoy doing and to ignore or cheat on the things we dislike. A course or test is like any other task before us—it should be completed as well as possible or not at all.

Blaming the test takers: The "everybody else is doing it" excuse doesn't fly for adults any more than it does for children. To begin with, everybody does not cheat. Only those with little self confidence think they have to cheat to succeed. Is it hard to see someone get a job or win an award dishonestly? Of course. But for every test taker who gets away with cheating there is one who is caught who, consequently, loses a lot—credit, reputation, trust, and possibly friendships. And the cheater ultimately must face the realization that eventually the cheat cheats himself.

Adult learners and test takers are probably less likely to feel the pressure to cheat than younger students. Many have been successful in life and in work and have lived long enough to have some perspective as to where test taking fits in the larger scheme of things. On the other hand, older learners may feel pulled in several directions at once, between work and family obligations. They do have time constraints and differing needs for a particular kind of course or exam. They may tend to regard the test as a necessary nuisance and simply choose the most expedient way for dealing with that nuisance—cheating. Or any age learner may just feel scared and insecure taking a test. Whatever the "reasons," the consequences of cheating on a test go far beyond the test itself. No test, no job, no grade in the world is worth the loss of one's personal moral compass.

What do you do if you see someone cheating? Whether you report a cheater to the instructor is something of a personal moral decision. It may depend on how sure you are of the incident and how strongly you feel about honesty other than your own. If your school or program has an honor system, you may want to read it carefully and understand it completely. If there is no institutional policy regarding the reporting of cheats, you must decide for yourself what action you want to take.

IN SHORT

Getting your mind and body in shape before your test will improve your chances for success. To be at your best, you need to get adequate sleep and exercise, eat well, and cut down on caffeine and cigarettes before the test.

PRE-TEST DIET AND EXERCISE PLAN

Fill out the following form to help you plan for your physical preparation before the exam.

The times of the day I am most alert are

_____

_____

The times of the day I am least alert are

_____

_____

In order to get 8 hours of rest each day, I should sleep during these times

_____

_____

When I study I like to eat

_____

_____

Three changes I will make in my diet prior to taking my test include

_____

_____

_____

My three days of exercise will include these activities

_____

_____

I will limit my drug intake to

_____cigarettes per week

_____alcoholic drinks per week

_____servings of caffeine (in soda or coffee) per day

PRE-TEST DIET AND EXERCISE PLAN

(Completed sample)

The times of the day I am most alert are
the morning and between 4:00 pm–6:00 pm

The times of the day I am least alert are
right after I get up, between 1:00 pm–3:00 pm and after 8:00 pm

In order to get 8 hours of rest each day, I should sleep during these times
10:30 pm–6:00 am and take naps on the weekends

When I study I like to eat
chips and crackers

Three changes I will make in my diet prior to taking my test include
eat apples and carrots instead of chips
cut down on coffee—only one cup in the morning
cut down on soda—only one can in the afternoon

My three days of exercise will include these activities
speed-walking and biking

I will limit my drug intake to
_____0_____ cigarettes per week
_____4_____ alcoholic drinks per week
_____2_____ servings of caffeine (in soda or coffee) per day

CHAPTER | 7

How do you juggle test preparation when you have so much to do and think about? How do you study for more than one test at a time? It's not always easy, but this chapter will show you how to make the most of your time and energy when tests are looming.

MANAGING STUDY SCHEDULES

L ike death, taxes, and childbirth, tests often come at inconvenient times. Test times are usually set by others, and you have little control over when you must sit for an exam. What you do have control over, though, is how you deal with the time you do have to prepare and how you juggle your other responsibilities around your test taking.

OCCASIONAL TESTS

Standardized tests—SATs and GEDs, for example—and civil service tests are given at a few set times of the year. This means that you can sometimes choose the test date that suits you best. In the case of some civil service tests and tests for some licenses, the exams are only given periodically and not on any particular schedule. You have to find out how and when such test dates are announced, and be ready to take the test whenever it is given.

There are advantages to taking exams that are scheduled some distance apart.

- You usually have the benefit of having a long preparation period.
- You are usually only preparing for one test at a time.
- The requirements for the test are usually fairly uniform. You know what to expect on the exam.

But there are drawbacks to periodically scheduled tests, too.

- If you miss a test, it may be a long time before you can take it again.
- Too much time ahead of the exam may encourage you to wait until the last minute to prepare.
- There isn't any leeway on when or where you can take the test. It has to be taken under standard testing conditions at a specific date, time, and location.

TESTS THAT ARE CLUSTERED TOGETHER

When it comes to taking academic tests, you face a different kind of time schedule. In the majority of courses, test dates are announced at the beginning of the semester in the course outline. Sometimes you get lucky; the test dates are neatly spaced out over the semester. But more often, there are peak times for tests—at mid-term and at the end of the semester—when you have several tests within days of each other.

Some of the advantages of taking classroom tests are

- You have access to the instructor to ask questions about the test.
- You generally have enough—but not too much—notice about test dates.
- There may be some flexibility in the schedule. An instructor might allow you to take an exam with another class that meets at a more convenient time for you, for example.

The disadvantages of classroom tests include

- During a few heavy exam times in the school year, the tests are scheduled close together, making study intense and often stressful.
- You must set priorities and decide which exams get more of your study time, based on course difficulty and its importance to your major and grade point average.

SPECIAL CHALLENGES FOR ADULT TEST TAKERS

Most likely, you're not *just* studying for tests. You might have lots of family responsibilities to deal with daily, or you might have a full-time job—or you might have both. Whatever else is going on in your life, you have a lot of juggling to do and a lot of demands on your time, concentration, and energy.

The stress you face can be considerable, whether you're taking a full-course load, or only a class or two at a time. With a full-time load of three, four, or more courses you may be facing a test almost every week. That means that you're in test preparation mode most of the time.

If you're taking only a course or two in addition to work and family responsibilities, you may find it difficult to shift gears into test preparation, because such studying has little to do with the rest of your life. Your school work and studying for tests is a separate set of activities and often takes a back seat to the more familiar chores of the day-to-day.

As a part-time student, or even a full-load commuting student, you're probably not as much a part of the class network as full-time, on-campus students are. That means you don't get as much news about instructors' preferences, test formats, and insider test information from former students in the class. You have to prepare for tests away from the support and assistance of other students.

A study group might be just what you need to help you stay focused and motivated and to keep you plugged into the class information network (see Chapter 3).

AVOIDING TIME CRUNCHES

Time management is especially important when you're gearing up for an exam. Here are some strategies that will help you use your time most effectively.

BUY A CALENDAR—AND LIVE BY IT

Actually, you should buy *two* calendars: a wall calendar and a pocket calendar. Having both will enable you to see the big picture and have a portable version with you at all times.

A Wall Calendar

On the wall calendar, write the dates of every upcoming test you know about. The monthly format should make it possible to see how your exams are clustered. Seeing heavy test traffic around specific weeks in the month will be a signal that you're going to have to factor in extra study time the weeks *before* those traffic jams. You should also fill in—in a different ink color—all the important dates in your home and work schedules. Then you'll be able to step back and see the whole month laid out in front of you.

A Pocket Calendar

There are several kinds of pocket calendars that offer daily, weekly, or monthly formats. The *monthly* format has similar advantages to the monthly wall calendar: It shows the whole month at a glance and lets you see exactly where there are periods of peak activity. The problem with a weekly calendar, though it has larger spaces to write in and allows you to be more complete in your entries, is that it doesn't show you what's coming up *next* week, for which you should be studying *now!*

Keep your pocket calendar with you all the time, so you can check on upcoming dates whenever you need to. You can also write in new dates as you get them, and then transfer them to your wall calendar when you get home.

ANTICIPATE TIME CONFLICTS

Imagine that you have a test in late November right after your Thanksgiving weekend at Aunt Dot's. And your final is just two days after you get back from that Chicago business trip. The timing's not good, but at least you know about the tests in advance and can plan accordingly. You can do most of your studying before you leave town. It's inevitable that there will be conflicts—life goes on, test or no test. Accept the fact that many things are going to come up at home or at work over which you have no control. Learn to get out in front of the things you do know about that can get in the way of your study plan.

ALWAYS FACTOR IN EXTRA TIME

You know those people who keep their clocks set five minutes ahead to assure that they will always arrive on time? Well, you can be like that; you can keep your "study clock" set ahead. If a test is going to be given on the 12th, mark the 10th as the date you want to be ready for the test. Whenever possible, build in a day or two of extra time to prepare for a test. A couple of days in the bank, so to speak, will be your insurance policy, to guard against getting sick, having to deal at the last minute with a work or family crisis, or other unforeseen difficulty that could eat into your study time and jeopardize your success on a test.

STUDY SMARTS FOR CLASSROOM TESTS

- **Finish all outstanding work first.** While you are typing the paper, completing the lab report, and reviewing for the quiz, start the preliminary steps for exam preparation, like gathering your notes and making study cards.
- **Study unlike subjects together.** Study math and English at one session and Spanish and science in another. You will be less likely to confuse information.
- **Study where you study best.** Work as much as possible in the library where distractions will be at a minimum.

TRIAGE: WHEN TIME IS RUNNING OUT

Uh oh, that test is coming up soon, and you're beginning to get tense. Despite your planning, you find yourself faced with just too little time to do what needs to be done to really be prepared.

Times like this call for what medical people call *triage.* In a triage unit, nurses and doctors tend the most serious cases first. When you are faced with several exams at once or with less time than you would like to prepare for one big test, you have to decide which part of the study plan needs the most immediate attention and the largest commitment of your time.

TRIAGE DURING CLASSROOM EXAM WEEK

When you're faced with three or more tests in one week, you may have to decide which courses, or which portions of a given course, you're going to concentrate on. Here are the steps you should take:

1. Make an honest appraisal of where you stand in each course. Make a list of the grades you think you would have in the classes before final exams.

2. Check your exam schedule. Your study schedule will depend in part on whether your exams are spaced evenly through the week or are clustered at the beginning or the end of it.

3. Write down what work needs to be done in each class before exam week (for example, you have a paper due in English, a lab report for your Biology class and a quiz in Spanish).

4. Look at your calendar and in pencil block out all times that are not available for study.

5. Go back and erase a few hours from your leisure time.

6. Looking at the white spaces left on your calendar, fill in review hours, starting with the course that has the lowest grade so far.

TRIAGE FOR A STANDARDIZED OR CIVIL SERVICE TEST

- Look at your calendar. Fill in all absolutely necessary obligations of work and family in pencil.

- Look again at the calendar. Erase at least two more things you can manage to do without or put off until after the test (maybe it's holiday shopping, housework, or a party).

- Arrange for a temporary substitute for outside activities you're involved in (maybe it's finding a sub for your place in the bowling league or on a PTA committee).

- Say no to new requests for your time. *Be tough about this.* There are not too many opportunities in life that won't be available later on.

- Enlist your family's support. Let them know what times of the day or night you need to study for the test. Get them to do the cooking and chores. Reward their support with thanks. Remind them—and yourself—that this is a short-term situation. Life will be normal again when the test is over. Be sure that you're willing to help them out in a stressful time as well.

- Assess your strengths and weaknesses in each of the areas that the test will cover. Take practice tests and write down questions that you find difficult. If you know that math, for example, is a weakness, arrange to spend some time with another student or a tutor to clarify topics you have forgotten.

STUDY SMARTS FOR A BIG TEST

Spend extended study time—an hour or more per session—doing practice tests and making study notes. Take your study notes, especially your flashcards, with you everywhere. Review them whenever you have five or fifteen minutes free. You'll be surprised how those small sessions add up. Ask someone—a family member, co-worker, or friend—to quiz you on your notes occasionally.

WHEN TIME HAS RUN OUT: CRAMMING

What do you do if you're down to the wire and have no choice but to try to stuff a lot of material in your head in the very short time that's left before your test? You have to cram, of course. Cramming is not a study strategy but rather Band-Aid surgery to do as good a job as you can on the test.

If cram you must, here are some suggestions for getting the most from your few precious hours:

- Choose a small number of topics, ideas, or facts that you think are the most important to know. Don't even try to master an entire term's worth of work at this point. Pick out only those topics you are confident will be on the exam.
- Repeat, repeat, repeat. Use all of your senses. Write the information. Say it out loud. Use highlighter pens to make important facts more visual.
- Outline and map as much information as you can (see Chapter 4). These techniques give you strong visual cues that may help you to remember the facts.
- Make flashcards on index cards and carry them around with you. Make the most of every spare minute you have.

On pages 85–86 you'll find two Triage Tactics—planners for organizing your study for classroom, civil service, and standardized tests. After you fill your answers in, check them against the two sample completed forms. Obviously, your answers will be different, but the samples will give you a good idea if your own answers are complete.

IN SHORT

You can successfully manage your study schedule by planning ahead, avoiding time crunches, using a wall and pocket calendar, and factoring in extra study time before the test. If time is running out and you need to cram for a test, block out every spare moment for studying, choose a small number of topics to focus on, repeat material aloud, and carry study note cards with you to study throughout the day.

TRIAGE TACTICS FOR A FINAL EXAM WEEK WITH TWO TO FOUR EXAMS SCHEDULED

Courses in which I will have a final exam

Course Name	Grade to date

Course work yet to be completed

_____

_____

_____

My exam schedule for finals week is as follows:

Day of the Week	Exam	Time
Monday		
Tuesday		
Wednesday		
Thursday		
Friday		

The exam that I need to spend the most time on is

_____

The exam that I need to spend the least time on is

_____

Three strategies I learned from this chapter that I will use to prepare for tests are

_____

_____

_____

TRIAGE TACTICS FOR PREPARING FOR A CIVIL SERVICE OR STANDARDIZED TEST

Three things I can take off my calendar to give me more time to prepare for the test are

_____

_____

_____

Three things I will ask my family, co-workers, or friends to do to help me are

_____

_____

_____

Based on my first practice test, the main areas I need to review are

_____

_____

My study goals for each of the next four weeks are
Week one:
_____

Week two:
_____

Week three:
_____

Week four:
_____

TRIAGE TACTICS FOR A FINAL EXAM WEEK WITH TWO TO FOUR EXAMS SCHEDULED

(Completed Sample)

Courses in which I will have a final exam

Course Name	Grade To Date
Biology 101	B+
English composition	C
Intro to Psych	A-
Math 101	B

Course work yet to be completed

bio labs 4 and 6

biographical essay for English

My exam schedule for finals week is as follows:

Day of the Week	Exam	Time
Monday	English comp	9:00 am
Tuesday	Biology	11:00 am
Wednesday	Math	2:30 pm
Thursday		
Friday	Psych	1:00 pm

The exam that I need to spend the most time on is

English Composition

The exam that I need to spend the least time on is

Intro to Psych

Three strategies I learned from this chapter that I will use to prepare for tests are

Carry around study notes for short-term study

Use a monthly calendar to keep track of time

Start early to review

TRIAGE TACTICS FOR PREPARING FOR A CIVIL SERVICE OR STANDARDIZED TEST
(Completed Sample)

Three things I can take off my calendar to give me more time to prepare for the test are
clothing drive committee
bowling on Tuesday nights
Sunday shopping with my sister

Three things I will ask my family, co-workers, or friends to do to help me are
Do food shopping on Saturday mornings
Take the dog to the vet
Screen phone calls in the evening while I'm studying

Based on my first practice test, the main areas I need to review are
reading comprehension
math problem solving

My study goals for each of the next four weeks are
Week one:
review one hour a day, five days a week

Week two:
meet with my study group for brainstorming

Week three:
concentrate on the hardest skills for me

Week four:
make a time plan for the last week of study

CHAPTER | 8

Exam days are stressful, but there are things you can do to cut down on stress. When the big day finally arrives, you'll be ready to face it in an organized and systematic way if you follow the advice here.

MANAGING TEST DAYS

Before a test in school when you were young, your mother probably told you to eat a good breakfast, sharpen your pencils, and relax. Good advice, to be sure.

But such simple advice isn't enough anymore because your life is a lot more complicated now. Breakfast may be a quick cup of coffee and a doughnut eaten on your way out the door to work, pencils may be in scarce supply because the whole family makes off with the ones left by the phone, and relaxation is hard won in the midst of family and job responsibilities.

You don't have the luxury of running off steam after a big test by racing around the playground or shooting hoops in the gym like school children, either. And you probably can't come home after a difficult exam to milk and cookies in front of the television. Your test days will be similar to any other days, filled with home and work responsibilities—only they will have the added anxiety of having to take a test.

When you were young, poor performance on a test might have meant you failed a course or got a bad mark on your report card. Troubling, to be sure, but only temporary. Tests that you take now, whether they're for a new job, higher education, or advanced vocational training, can carry much larger consequences. You may have to make considerable sacrifices of time and energy to prepare for one of them. It makes sense, then, not to risk it all by falling apart on test day.

EARLY IN THE DAY
BUILD IN LOTS OF TIME FOR YOURSELF

Even if your test is early in the morning, be sure that you have more than enough time to be settled in the examining room before the test. This may take some extra planning.

- **Get up early.** Set two alarm clocks to be sure that you don't oversleep. If you are a heavy sleeper, ask someone to rouse you personally or to call your house to make sure you are awake.
- **Double-check the location and time of the test.** Write it down where you can see it, so the information doesn't get misplaced.
- **Get as much ready the night before as you can.** Have your clothing ready to jump into if necessary. Make sure there is gas in the car, or get your public transportation fare ready the night before the test.
- **Know exactly where you're going.** Know the most reliable route for getting to the test site. Check ahead of time on the location and cost of parking. If possible, make a trial run to the testing location a week or so before the test so you know about how long the drive or trip will take you. Check out alternate ways of getting to the testing site in case you run into car trouble, accidents, road construction, or breakdowns in public transportation. Have a neighbor, co-worker, or family member ready to help you out in the event of one of these emergencies.

FEEL GOOD

To do a good job on the test, you have to feel good, both mentally and physically.

- **Stay healthy**. Be especially careful of your health near exam time; stay away from people who have been sick. If you must tend a sick child or family member, do your best to keep germs at bay by taking some simple precautions like washing your hands frequently and keeping food and drink utensils separate.
- **Sleep well**. The night before a test is not a good night to stay out late or overindulge in food or drink. The morning after these activities is not a good morning to take a test.
- **Dress comfortably**. Choose an outfit to wear for the test that you really like and that feels good on you. If you have a lucky color or lucky outfit, wear it. It can't hurt! Dress in layers. You don't know what the temperature of the testing room may be. At any time of the year the room could be ice cold or stifling hot. If you wear a sweater, you can take it off if it's stuffy or put it on if it's chilly. If you wear all heavy or light clothing, you can't compensate for the differences in temperature.
- **Eat lightly, but nutritionally.** Test day is probably not a good day to eat a big plate of steak and eggs early in the morning. A heavy meal before a test may make you sleepy or sluggish. A breakfast of cereal, fruit, or yogurt, or a simple sandwich and soup for lunch before a test, will make you feel fueled for the test but not loaded down with extra baggage.
- **Exercise moderately.** If exercise relaxes or energizes you, build in time for your morning run or brisk walk before leaving for the test. But refrain from doing a heavy workout. Do some mild exercise instead; it can be very helpful in relieving stress and contributing to feelings of well-being.
- **Don't drink a lot**. If the test is a long test, don't drink a lot of coffee or soda before the test. Most tests don't have bathroom breaks!
- **Think positive**. Think positively about your preparation for the test and *look forward to doing well.*

MAKE SURE YOU HAVE THE SUPPLIES YOU NEED

Remember to take those sharp pencils—and anything else you will need during the test—with you.

- **Take admissions materials.** If there are admission cards or documents you must take to the exam, be sure you have them ready and handy on the morning of the test.
- **Limit your study materials.** Take the minimum of study cards or notes with you. Don't carry your texts or review books to the testing site. You will be tempted to look at them and panic when you can't remember something that you run across in the text. By the time you are ready to take the test, your notes should be boiled down to just the few you want to review very briefly right before.
- **Take extra pens and pencils.** Pens might leak; pencils might break—so bring a couple of extras just in case.
- **Wear a watch.** Make sure it is working.
- **Take chewing gum or mints to munch on.** They will prevent your mouth from getting dry and can be refreshing.
- **Take a pack of tissues.** You can't think when your nose is running.
- **Take good luck with you.** If you are so inclined, put your lucky charm, worry beads, or other comfort item in your pocket or bag.

AT THE TESTING SITE

So far, so good. When you get to the testing site, here are some things you can do to ensure that you do your best.

15 MINUTES BEFORE THE TEST

You should be at or in sight of the examining room 15 minutes before the test. Then you should

- **Chat amiably with other test takers.** Resist the temptation to ask about how long they prepared or how they feel about the test. If you think that they're better prepared or more confident than you are, you might get more nervous. Talk about the weather instead.
- **Try not to compare notes.** Don't worry about what other people know—or think they know—about the test. If someone mentions that he or she thinks that there will be questions on some topic you never heard of, all you will be able to think about is that topic, and in your panic you may lose your grip on information you *do* have

in your head. If that subject is indeed on the test, deal with it then. There's nothing you can do about learning it now, and chances are it won't be on the test anyway.

- **Put away your notes and review sheets.** Think good thoughts about what life will be like after the test is over. Remind yourself that any test, short of some serious medical test, is not a matter of life and death. You will survive.

WITH THE TEST IN FRONT OF YOU

Don't jump the gun! Though you may be very anxious to get started on the test, resist the temptation to start working before all instructions have been given. Pay particular attention to such things as

- **How to fill out the answer sheets.** You may have a seat number or testing number that needs to be included or personal data that is required on the test. For example, test forms often ask for your date of birth (DOB). Remember not to write in the day of the test instead. Examiners might be impressed that an apparent newborn scored so well on the test, but more likely they will want you to correct your mistake.
- **How to change answers.** There are often specific rules about changing answers on test papers. Make sure you know how to change your mind without losing points.
- **Time limits.** You need to know how long you have for the test and whether there will be a break.
- **Can you write in the test booklet?** You'll want to know if you're permitted to work on scratch paper or to make marks in the test booklet. This is critical if you are to use some of the strategies suggested later in this book.

Be confident! When you first look at the test, take a deep breath and approach it with a take-charge attitude. Who is the boss here? The test—which is flat and lifeless—or you, who's an adult and ready to succeed?

WHEN THE TEST IS OVER

Look the instructor in the eye with a smile on your face as you hand in your paper. If he or she remembers that you seemed confident, that person may approach the reading of your paper with a positive attitude toward you. It can't hurt. Once outside the testing room, don't have any post-test conversation with other students. It isn't going to help you to compare notes on an experience that is already over.

Then, if possible, go home and relax. Take a run or a walk to unwind. Treat yourself to a snack, a hot shower, or a half an hour of mindless TV. Go bowling or to a movie. Test taking can be exhausting. If you've prepared long and hard, you deserve a break. Take it while you can.

On the following page is an exercise that will get you thinking about your approaching test day. Read each problem in the first column and match it with the best solution in the second column. When you're done, see how well you did by checking your answers against the answer sheet that follows.

IN SHORT

You can confidently manage your test day by waking up early, eating right, dressing comfortably, and thinking positively. Bring extra pens and pencils, a watch, tissues, and admission tickets with you to the test site. Don't discuss the test with others beforehand, or you may get nervous about your preparation level. Listen carefully to all the instructions before you begin the test, and find out if you can write in the test booklet or on scratch paper during the test.

BE READY WHEN TEST DAY COMES

Match the test-day problems in column A with their solutions in column B.

Column A

___ 1. I am a heavy sleeper. I am afraid I'll oversleep on test day.

___ 2. The test is in another part of town I don't know well.

___ 3. I'm really stressed about this test. I feel sick to my stomach and can't sleep.

___ 4. I have been sick for nearly a week and haven't been able to study.

___ 5. Another student in my class wants me to meet an hour before the test to study.

___ 6. I don't want to take all of my books on the long bus ride across town to the test.

___ 7. It's been years since I took a test like this. How will I know what to do?

___ 8. After I get my kids off to school, I will have time for a good breakfast or a run before I leave. Which is more important?

___ 9. I'm afraid I won't have time to do all the essays because I am a slow writer.

___10. A classmate wants me to review with her after the exam.

Column B

a. Bring to the test only your study notes and cards.

b. Set two alarms and ask a friend to call you.

c. Take your run and get a bit to eat—coffee and a roll—once you get near the exam site.

d. Unless you need coaching on a specific skill, avoid last-minute study with someone else.

e. Make a time schedule for the essays before you begin work on them. Try to stay on track throughout the test.

f. Listen to oral instructions very carefully. Ask questions if you don't understand any part of the directions.

g. Don't fret about lost time. Add in a little extra study time every day.

h. Rather than rehash the test right after the exam, take a break from the test.

i. Take a test run to the exam site a few days before the test.

j. Try relaxation or exercise techniques to overcome severe test anxiety. Stay healthy.

BE READY WHEN TEST DAY COMES

(Answer Sheet)

Column A

_b_ 1. I am a heavy sleeper. I am afraid I'll oversleep on test day.

_i_ 2. The test is in another part of town I don't know well.

_j_ 3. I'm really stressed about this test. I feel sick to my stomach and can't sleep.

_g_ 4. I have been sick for nearly a week and haven't been able to study.

_d_ 5. Another student in my class wants me to meet an hour before the test to study.

_a_ 6. I don't want to take all of my books on the long bus ride across town to the test.

_f_ 7. It's been years since I took a test like this. How will I know what to do?

_c_ 8. After I get my kids off to school, I will have time for a good breakfast or a run before I leave. Which is more important?

_e_ 9. I'm afraid I won't have time to do all the essays because I am a slow writer.

_h_ 10. A classmate wants me to review with her after the exam.

Column B

a. Bring to the test only your study notes and cards.

b. Set two alarms and ask a friend to call you.

c. Take your run and get a bit to eat—coffee and a roll—once you get near the exam site.

d. Unless you need coaching on a specific skill, avoid last-minute study with someone else.

e. Make a time schedule for the essays before you begin work on them. Try to stay on track throughout the test.

f. Listen to oral instructions very carefully. Ask questions if you don't understand any part of the directions.

g. Don't fret about lost time. Add in a little extra study time every day.

h. Rather than rehash the test right after the exam, take a break from the test.

i. Take a test run to the exam site a few days before the test.

j. Try relaxation or exercise techniques to overcome severe test anxiety. Stay healthy.

CHAPTER | 9

In this chapter, you will learn how to deal with the most common type of exam question—the multiple-choice question. This chapter introduces the multiple-choice format and deals with questions requiring recall or recognition of material. Chapter 10 deals with other specific kinds of multiple-choice questions.

PSYCHING OUT THE MULTIPLE-CHOICE TEST

Test questions are geared to tap in to your knowledge of subject matter or to measure your skills at performing some task. Some test questions require you to *recall* specific items of information; others ask you only to *recognize* information by separating it from similar choices. And still others have you reason out answers based on text presented in the test itself. All of these kinds of questions are most frequently presented in a multiple-choice format in which you must choose the one best answer.

Generally speaking, multiple-choice questions are considered to be *objective* questions because they are based solely on the information; they don't allow for the opinion or interpretation of the test taker.

WHY MULTIPLE-CHOICE?

Multiple-choice is the most popular format for most standardized, civil service, and certificate or licensure tests. There are two reasons for this:

- Like most short answer tests, they are easier and quicker to grade.
- They do not penalize test takers who know the information but have poorly developed writing skills or problems with expressive language.

HOW THE QUESTIONS ARE WRITTEN

You may remember taking tests that contained questions like this one:

1. The largest of the Great Lakes is
- **a.** Huron
- **b.** Superior
- **c.** Erie
- **d.** Mississippi

The answer is **b**. This is a much simpler example than you would find on the SAT or a civil service test, but it does contain the three elements of most multiple-choice questions, which are stems, options, and distractors.

Stem:	"The largest of the Great Lakes is"
Options:	All answer choices
Distractors:	Incorrect answer choices

STEMS

Stems contain the information on which the question is based. In longer tests, the stems of the questions may be as long as a paragraph and could contain a lot of information that you must sift through before you can choose an answer.

Sometimes stem questions are phrased as *situations*. Situation questions set a scene or set of facts on which the test taker is required to answer a series of questions. Stems can also be simply a word, a math example, or a fragment of a sentence that serves to frame the question.

OPTIONS

Options are the answer choices offered to you, the test taker. Many options require that you simply recognize a correct choice among several others.

2. As President, Ronald Reagan came to be known as

    a. Old Hickory

    b. The Great Communicator

    c. Speaker of the House

    d. Old Ironsides

The answer is **b.**

Some test makers test the accuracy of your knowledge by offering two or more options that are similar.

3. The word in the following sentence that means the same or almost the same as *flammable* is

    a. fireproof

    b. fire resistant

    c. easily burned

    d. burning

It wouldn't be enough in this question that you know that *flammable* has something to do with fire. All of the options offer that choice. You have to know that the particular word pertaining to fire that you want means that something is easily burned, answer **c.**

DISTRACTORS

Distractors are the incorrect answers that offer a challenge to the test takers. In question 2, above, the distractors are **a, c,** and **d**; and in question 3, they are **a, b,** and **d.**

Distractors are often written to force test takers to be very careful in their selections. In question 2, for instance, if you didn't know that Reagan was known by the epithet *The Great Communicator,* you could be distracted by the two choices that refer to age. Since Reagan was one of our oldest presidents while in office, you might be tempted to choose one of them.

The wise test taker will eliminate the clearly impossible options first. In question 2, both *Old Ironsides,* which is the name of a ship, and *Speaker of the House,* which is an office that cannot be held by a sitting president, should be eliminated. Then, between *Old Hickory* and *The Great Communicator,* you would have to make a choice. If you remembered that *Old*

Hickory was the term used to describe President Andrew Jackson, you would eliminate it, and then the correct choice would be obvious.

RECOGNITION AND RECALL QUESTIONS

As noted before, multiple-choice questions force you to recall or recognize specific information that is surrounded by other similar but incorrect options. These other options can be written in such a way that they confuse the unwary or unwise test taker.

4. Choose the word or phrase that means the same or almost the same as the word *secession.*
   a. a meeting
   b. the act of breaking away from a political body
   c. a surgical birth
   d. a parade

5. Circle the word that is correctly spelled in the following group of words.
   a. chanel
   b. channel
   c. chanle
   d. chanell

6. Choose the correct punctuation from the choices below.
   I went to lunch with my two
   a. sister in laws
   b. sister-in-laws
   c. sister's in law
   d. sisters-in-law

In questions 4–6, you would have to rely on your memory for the definition of *secession,* the spelling of the word *channel,* and the plural forms for hyphenated words, or you would have to be able to recognize the correct answer in comparison to the other choices. The correct answers are: 4 is **b**, 5 is **b**, and 6 is **d**. Some strategies for approaching these kinds of questions are outlined next.

Let Your Eye Be Your Guide

Look at the four choices of spelling. Which *looks* like something you've seen before? (*channel*)

Let Your Ear Be Your Guide

Listen to the differences between *sister-in-laws* and *sisters-in-law*. Which sounds better? (*sisters-in-law*) You would have to remember the hyphen rule in this word, however.

Beware! Note distractors **c** and **d** in question 4. Many multiple-choice questions are designed to confuse you by offering options that sound like the stem word or have associations with the stem word. In this instance the similarity between *procession* and *secession,* and the distant but confusing sound similarities between *secession* and the medical short hand *C-section* for cesarean section could trap the unwary test taker.

Try Each Option as a True/False Question

"A secession is a meeting. True or false?" "A secession is an act of breaking away from a political body. True or false?" Which statement seems to make the most sense?

READING AND REASONING QUESTIONS

Some multiple-choice questions are geared to measure your ability to take information directly from the text and to answer questions based on that text. This format is almost always used in civil service tests, which are more concerned with how well you could be trained for a job than with specific knowledge you already possess. These kinds of multiple-choice questions typically measure reading comprehension.

Generally, reading comprehension tests start with a passage on a particular subject, followed by as few as two or as many as ten questions based on the content of that passage.

These questions usually are aimed at four skills:

1. Recognizing the *definition* of a vocabulary word in the passage
2. Identifying the *main idea* of the passage
3. Noting a specific *fact or detail* in the passage
4. Making an *inference or conclusion* based on information in the passage that is not directly stated

Read the following passage and the four questions that follow. Identify each type of question from the list above.

The "broken window" theory was originally developed to explain how minor acts of vandalism or disrespect can quickly escalate to crimes and attitudes that break down the entire social fabric of an area or unit. It is an idea that can easily be applied to any situation in society. The theory contends that if a broken window in an abandoned building is not replaced quickly, soon all the windows in that building will be broken.

In other words, a small violation, if condoned, leads others to commit similar or greater violations. Thus, after all the windows have been broken, the building is likely to be looted and perhaps even burned down. According to this theory, violations increase exponentially. Thus, if disrespect to a superior is tolerated, others will be tempted to be disrespectful as well. A management crisis could erupt literally overnight.

For example, if one firefighter begins to disregard proper housewatch procedure by neglecting to keep up the housewatch administrative journal, and this firefighter is not reprimanded, others will follow suit by committing similar violations of procedure, thinking, "If he can get away with it, why can't I?" So what starts out as a small thing, a violation that may seem not to warrant disciplinary action, may actually ruin the efficiency of the entire firehouse, putting the people the firehouse serves at risk.

7. In this passage the word *reprimanded* means
   a. scolded
   b. praised
   c. rewarded
   d. fired

Question type_____

8. The best title for this passage would be

  a. Broken Windows: Only the First Step

  b. The Importance of Housewatch

  c. How to Write an Administrative Journal

  d. A Guide to Window Repair

Question type_____

9. The passage suggests that

  a. firefighters are sloppy administrators

  b. firefighters will blame others for mistakes

  c. discipline starts with small infractions

  d. discipline is important for the efficiency of the firehouse

Question type_____

10. According to the passage, which of the following could be the result of broken windows?

  a. The building would soon be vandalized.

  b. Firefighters would lose morale.

  c. There could be a management crisis.

  d. The efficiency of the firehouse could be destroyed.

Question type_____

Answers

  7. a. *Reprimanded* means *scolded.* (Vocabulary)

  8. a. The passage is about the "broken window" theory, showing that a minor violation or breach of discipline can lead to major violations. (Main idea)

  9. d. The passage applies the broken window theory to firehouse discipline, showing that even small infractions have to be dealt with to avoid worse problems later. (Inference)

  10. a. See the third sentence of the passage. (Detail)

ANSWERING STRATEGIES

Answering many multiple-choice questions correctly requires either direct knowledge or recognition and recall of specific facts, or the ability to understand written information well enough to answer questions based on that written information.

A successful test taker will approach multiple-choice questions with several good strategies. They include:

1. Unless instructed not to write on the test paper, always circle or **underline the key words in the stem** that direct your search for the answer. In the earlier examples, *President* was the key word in question 2, and *the same or almost the same* were the key words in question 4.

2. **Eliminate immediately all clearly incorrect distractors.** This will usually mean that you have to choose between two similar choices.

3. **Beware of examiners' tricks to confuse you:** look-alike options, easily confused options, silly options. Watch for tricky wordings such as "All of the following are true *except . . . .*"

4. **Read stems carefully** to be sure you understand *exactly* what is being asked. You will find distractors that are accurate and may sound right but do not apply to that stem. This is particularly true of options that say "All of the above" or "none of the above."

5. **Be familiar with the kinds of questions that are asked on multiple-choice tests.** This way you can quickly identify what you are looking for in a question.

6. **Beware of the absolute!** Read carefully any stem that includes words like *always, never, none,* or *all.* An answer may sound perfectly correct and the general principal may be correct. However, it may not be true in all circumstances. For example, think about the statement "All roses are red." ALL roses?

7. **Do the easiest questions first.** Many tests are arranged so that the questions move from easy to more difficult. Don't lose out on easier points by skipping over those early questions and risk running out of time.

8. When answering questions with fairly lengthy stems, **read the**

Use Your Test Book!

Unless you are forbidden to write in your test book, make good use of the margins and white space to note questions, make diagrams, or do calculations. Underline, circle, and draw boxes around key words for phrases in the stem.

options before you read the stem. Then when you read the question, you will already know what information you are seeking.

On the following page, write one of each of the question types discussed in this chapter. If you can write one, you can answer one!

In Short

Most standardized, civil service, and certificate tests use the multiple-choice format for many questions. The three main elements of multiple-choice questions are stems, options, and distractors. Many multiple-choice questions measure reading comprehension. Strategies for answering multiple-choice questions include circling the key words in the stem of the questions, immediately eliminating all clearly incorrect distractors, and becoming familiar with the different kinds of questions that are asked.

TRY OUT YOUR MULTIPLE-CHOICE QUESTION SKILLS

Read the following passage. Then write one of each of the four types of multiple-choice questions, based on the content of the passage.

Detectives who routinely investigate violent crimes can't help but become somewhat jaded. Paradoxically, the victims and witnesses with whom they closely work are often in a highly vulnerable and emotional state. The emotional fallout from a sexual assault, for example, can be complex and long-lasting. Detectives must be trained to handle people in emotional distress and must be sensitive to the fact that for the victim the crime is not routine. At the same time, detectives must recognize the limits of their role and resist the temptation to act as therapists or social workers instead of referring victims to the proper agencies.

1. A main idea question

_____

_____

    a.

    b.

    c.

    d.

2. A detail question

_____

_____

    a.

    b.

    c.

    d.

3. A vocabulary question

_____

_____

    a.

    b.

    c.

    d.

4. An inference question

_____

_____

    a.

    b.

    c.

    d.

TRY OUT YOUR MULTIPLE-CHOICE QUESTION SKILLS
(Sample answers)

1. A main idea question

What is the main idea of the passage?

a. Detectives who investigate violent crime must never become emotionally hardened by the experience.

b. Victims of violent crime should be referred to therapists and social workers.

c. Detectives should be sensitive to the emotional state of victims of violent crime.

d. Detectives should be particularly careful in dealing with victims of sexual assault.

2. A detail question

Which of the following would be an appropriate response by a detective to a victim in emotional distress?

a. immediate assistance

b. a sympathetic ear

c. arrest of the perpetrator

d. referral to social service agencies

3. A vocabulary question

In this passage, the word "jaded" means

a. nervous

b. lazy

c. insensitive

d. hostile

4 An inference question

The passage suggests that police detectives

a. are often arrogant in dealing with victims

b. should be sympathetic to victims

c. have responsibilities beyond the arrest of criminals

d. are underpaid

CHAPTER | 10

How well can you read a
graph or chart? Answer
math questions? Make
a judgment call in an on-
the-job situation? Find out
in this chapter, as you pick
up new tips for dealing
with such test questions.

MORE MULTIPLE-
CHOICE
QUESTIONS

I n the last chapter you saw how multiple-
choice questions are designed to trigger your recall and recognition
of learned material. But multiple-choice questions can be used to
test other things as well.

Multiple-choice questions can test math skills because they can
require specific mastery of math operations, and they can require you
to choose answers that appear correct in comparison to other choices.
Multiple-choice questions can also determine how well you can read
graphs, maps, charts, and diagrams and pull information from them. In
civil service tests, you may also see questions that test your ability to use
good judgment and common sense in job-related situations.

MULTIPLE-CHOICE MATH QUESTIONS

Math questions appear on tests for a couple of reasons. In the GED or SAT, examiners may be looking for levels of competence or achievement in math. On civil service exams, the math questions are geared more toward assessing how a person applies basic math skills to workplace situations.

Some questions are mostly numerical in format:

1. What is the reciprocal of $3\frac{7}{8}$?
   a. $\frac{31}{28}$
   b. $\frac{8}{31}$
   c. $\frac{8}{21}$
   d. $\frac{31}{8}$

Some questions are introduced by stems in which the needed numerical information is embedded:

2. A city worker is paid time-and-a-half an hour in overtime pay. He earns $20 per hour. If he works four hours more than his contracted work week, how much does he make in overtime pay?
   a. $80.00
   b. $120.00
   c. $400.00
   d. $60.00

Answers

1. **b.** $3\frac{7}{8} = \frac{31}{8}$, whose reciprocal is $\frac{8}{31}$.
2. **b.** The worker makes $20 x $1\frac{1}{2}$ = $30 per hour in overtime. Now multiply the hourly overtime wage by the number of overtime hours: 30 x 4 = 120.

STRATEGIES FOR ANSWERING MATH QUESTIONS

Even though you're dealing with numbers and not words in math questions, the way you analyze the questions and consider the possible answers is very similar to the types of word questions you read about in Chapter 9.

- Don't panic because it's math; they're only numbers after all.
- Read the stem carefully. Underline or circle the most important information in the stem.
- Read all the options carefully. Don't be confused by look-alike numbers.
- Work the problem. If you see an answer that matches, you can move right on. Do all calculations on paper, not in your head.
- Skip unfamiliar questions on the first pass through the test. Put a dot in the margin of the test so you can locate the question quickly if you are in a hurry.
- Be careful when you write your calculations. The number 1 can look like 7, 3 like 8, and 6 like 0 when you are in a hurry. You risk picking up a wrong answer or wasting time recalculating an answer to find something that fits from your choice of answers.
- Translate numbers from math into English. (*Reciprocal* in question 1 means *the inverse of the fractional number.*)
- Translate words from English into math. (*Time and a half* in question 2 means $1\frac{1}{2}$ or $\frac{3}{2}$.)

QUESTIONS ABOUT GRAPHIC MATERIAL

Graphic material consists of maps, charts, graphs, illustrations, or diagrams that summarize a sizable amount of information in a compact, visual format. Like some math applications, questions based on graphic material are used to test the skill of the test taker in pulling information from non-verbal sources.

Being an adult probably gives you an advantage with this type of question. You're accustomed to seeing graphic material all the time: train, bus, and plane timetables; work, school, and recreation schedules; recipes; newspaper graphs; and maps. You have more experience than younger people in translating information from print sources such as these, and you're generally more accustomed to seeking guidance from graphics in your daily life.

If you're a weekend carpenter, you know how to follow building diagrams. If you coach Little League, you deal with team rosters and game schedules. Commuters must find their way to work despite confusing directions and public transportation schedules.

Below are two kinds of graphic representations similar to those that appear on civil service tests.

3. What is the percentage of smoking-related fires?
   a. 26
   b. 32
   c. 58
   d. 26–58

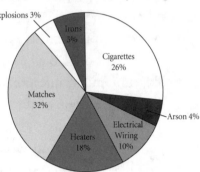

Causes of Household Fires, in percentages

Explosions 3%
Irons 5%
Cigarettes 26%
Matches 32%
Arson 4%
Electrical Wiring 10%
Heaters 18%

4. Based on the information provided in the chart, which of the following reasons applies to the majority of these fires?
   a. malicious intent to harm
   b. violation of fire safety codes
   c. carelessness
   d. faulty products

5. At which point does the rate of increase of sick days change?
   a. 4 years of employment
   b. 10 years of employment
   c. 8 years of employment
   d. 12 years of employment

Number of Sick Days Per Year of Employment

Number of Years of Eployment

Number of Paid Sick Days

Answers

3. **d.** Both cigarettes (26 percent) and matches (32 percent) are smoking related, but not all match fires are necessarily smoking related. So the best answer allows for a range between 26 and 58 percent.

4. **c.** Fires from cigarettes, heaters, irons, and matches—81 percent in all—are the most likely the result of carelessness.

5. **b.** At ten years of employment, the rate of increase goes up from two days every two years to four days every two years.

STRATEGIES FOR ANSWERING GRAPHIC QUESTIONS

- Don't rush to choose your answer; spend a few minutes really analyzing each graphic first.
- Translate the components of the graphic—axes on a line graph, slices of a pie chart, for example—into their verbal counterpart (for example, from the graphics here, causes of household fires, or numbers of sick days per year of employment).
- Read all options carefully.
- Think about how the information shown in the graphic makes sense in real-life terms. Should paid sick leave be tied to number of years employed? What *would* be the major causes of household fires?
- Remember that these are good questions. You don't have to have specific information before you come to the test. Everything you need is given to you in the graphic.

JUDGMENT QUESTIONS

So far you have learned about kinds of multiple-choice questions that rely on recognizing or recalling information. There is yet another very common kind of question, especially on civil service exams, that allows the test taker to demonstrate not only job skills, but also personal skills.

These are questions that require you to use common sense and judgment to identify the correct option. They don't require knowledge of the job. The test makers are interested in how well you understand the overall requirements of the job—a job, for example, in clerical work, nursing, law enforcement, firefighting, or sanitation.

Civil service employers are concerned with your ability to react appropriately in an emergency, to represent the agency or department to the public, and to follow rules and regulations. Judgment and common-sense questions require that you think like a police officer, firefighter, sanitation worker, or postal clerk.

That's not so easy to do if you have never been one of those things. However, you should have a general sense of appropriate behavior in situations that require on-the-job decision making. Common sense and good judgment are assets you probably have a lot of, and this is another advantage you have over younger people.

- You have the awareness of what is expected of workers in various fields.
- You have the maturity to gauge the impact of your behavior on others.
- You have the life experience to see how your actions affect other people.

In general, common-sense and judgment questions are concerned with a few basic issues:
- Safety for workers and the public
- Courtesy and public relations; workers represent the department in the community
- Adherence to regulations that reduce risks of damage, lawsuits, and other problems arising from failure to follow rules

Below are samples of judgment questions that are similar to those on civil service tests.

6. The rain from last night has frozen, and you are operating a salt spreader. You see a sign just before you get to a bridge. The sign reads *Bridge Freezes Before Roadway.* What should you do?
   a. speed up to get over the bridge before your tires slide
   b. drive slowly while spreading the salt in case the bridge has ice on it
   c. park the truck at the side of the road and wait for assistance
   d. pump the brakes as you drive over the bridge in order to avoid a skid

7. A neighborhood woman enters the firehouse and asks you to cut down a tree in her yard because it is too close to the utility lines. She claims that this is a fire hazard so you should handle it. You should
   a. get the ax and chop the tree down
   b. tell her to call her utility company so that it can handle the problem properly
   c. refuse her request but tell her your brother will do it for $50
   d. tell her to stop bothering the fire department unless there is a fire

When called upon to work a collision scene, a police officer should do the following things in this order:

a. Have all drivers move all vehicles not in need of a tow truck out of the roadway.

b. Position the patrol car behind disabled vehicles to keep other traffic from becoming involved.

c. Turn on emergency lights so other traffic is warned of the problem.

d. Call tow trucks if needed.

e. Put on reflective traffic vest if traffic direction becomes necessary.

f. Have the drivers, passengers, and witnesses step out of the roadway.

g. Collect information from drivers, passengers, and witnesses.

8. Officer Gofort has been dispatched to a four-car collision at Maple and Walnut. When he arrives he notices that all four cars are in the same lane of traffic and have apparently run into the back of each other. What is the first thing he should do?

a. call for four tow trucks to be en route to his location

b. have the drivers move all cars not in need of a tow into a nearby parking lot

c. put on his reflective vest

d. collect information from all drivers, passengers, and witnesses

Answers

6. b. The sign is telling you there might be ice on the bridge, so caution is in order—but not excessive caution, as in answer **c.**

7. b. The utility company should handle this problem. You should not handle the problem on your own (answer **a**), and the other two choices don't reflect well on your employer, the fire department.

8. b. This is the first step in the procedure given.

STRATEGIES FOR ANSWERING JUDGMENT QUESTIONS

Answer judgment questions just as you would multiple-choice questions (discussed in Chapter 9) that are based on reading passages of text. Begin by reading the stem of the question carefully, but don't overanalyze it.

- Imagine yourself in the situation described in the question, and think about how you would act. If your response is based on common sense or on information in the question itself, it is probably correct.
- Keep in mind the need to follow procedures that will ensure safety and security.
- When given a stem that offers information on regulations or procedures, followed by a group of questions, make sure you underline the key aspects of the question that support your choice of options.
- Trust yourself. These are the kinds of questions adults answer best. Deal from your strength!

On the following page you have an opportunity to practice answering the kinds of questions you might find on tests that include sections on math, graphics, and making decisions in fairly typical on-the-job situations.

IN SHORT

Multiple-choice math, graphic, and judgment questions are similar to the multiple-choice word questions discussed in Chapter 9. Strategies for approaching the questions include translating numbers from math into English, doing all calculations on paper, and reading the stem of the question carefully. Use your common sense and life experience to help you answer judgment questions.

TEST IT OUT

Answer the following sample multiple-choice questions in math, graphics, and judgment.

1. A sanitation worker earns a salary of $28,000 per year. This year he will earn a 3% raise. What is his new salary?
   a. $840
   b. $28,540
   c. $37,300
   d. $28,840

2. The speed limit on Maple Drive is 30 mph. The speed limit on the expressway is $1\frac{1}{2}$ times faster than the Maple Drive limit. What is the speed limit on the expressway?
   a. 65 mph
   b. 15 mph
   c. 45 mph
   d. 20 mph

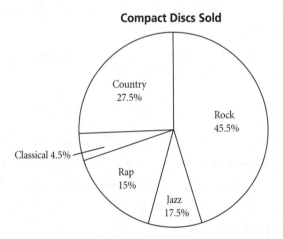

Compact Discs Sold

Country 27.5%

Rock 45.5%

Classical 4.5%

Rap 15%

Jazz 17.5%

3. Which types of music represent exactly half of the compact disks sold?
   a. Rock and jazz
   b. Classical and rock
   c. Rap, classical, and country
   d. Jazz, country, and rap

4. A sanitation truck stops for a collection at a city park. The worker sees trash strewn around the area of the container. Regulations say that sanitation workers are only responsible for trash inside the containers. Because of the public nature of the location, workers are concerned for the well being of people in the park. They should
   a. leave the trash on the ground
   b. call the supervisor for permission to pick up the trash
   c. pick up the trash and work more quickly to make up the time
   d. leave the trash on the ground and report the incident to the supervisor after the run

5. A group of school children is visiting a firehouse as part of a class trip. One child misbehaves and climbs on the fire truck and handles apparatus in defiance of the firefighter conducting the tour. The firefighter should then
   a. ask the class to leave the station
   b. ignore the child
   c. reprimand the child so that the child will understand proper behavior
   d. escort the child to the teacher and explain the dangers posed by bad behavior in the station

Answers

1. **d.** Multiply the salary by 3 percent, or .03: 28,000 x .03 = 840. Now add this increase to the original salary to get $28,840.
2. **c.** Multiply 30 by $1\frac{1}{2}$, or $\frac{3}{2}$, to get 45 miles per hour.
3. **b.** Rock is 45.5% and classical 4.5%.
4. **b.** Always consult your supervisor for approval of any change in your work order.
5. **d.** The teacher, not the firefighter, is responsible for the children's behavior. However, the firefighter should not allow this misbehavior to continue, since it may endanger the child or people who might later depend on the performance of the apparatus.

CHAPTER | 11

Not all short-answer
questions on all classroom
tests are multiple-choice.
In this chapter, you'll read
about other questions that
you'll probably encounter,
and discover ways
to analyze them and
increase your chances of
getting them right.

QUESTIONS ON THE CLASSROOM TEST

While multiple-choice questions are
the ones that usually come to mind when you think about
tests, classroom exams are usually made up of a variety of
short questions. Different formats test different types of information
and various ways of demonstrating skills and knowledge.

WHAT QUESTIONS CAN YOU EXPECT?

You have seen that most test questions on standardized and civil service
tests are based on the multiple-choice format. In the classroom,
however, there are a number of question formats that are commonly

used along with or instead of multiple-choice questions to allow an examiner to determine how much you are learning in a course.

RECOGNITION QUESTIONS

There are two types of recognition questions:

- True/false—tell whether the statements represent accurate or inaccurate information
- Matching two lists—match the words or terms in the first column with those that most apply in the second.

RECALL QUESTIONS

There are three kinds of recall questions:

- Completions—supply words needed to complete the idea of the statement or sentence
- Identifications—define words, terms, or names from memory
- Essays—develop extended answers, usually one or more paragraphs, from your own knowledge of the topic. (Essay writing is covered in Chapters 14–16.)

WHY SO MANY KINDS OF QUESTIONS?

Unlike writers of standardized and civil service exams, an individual class teacher can construct tests to suit individual goals, both philosophical and practical.

PHILOSOPHICAL PURPOSES

Teachers want to make sure that tests do a good job of testing many things.

- A variety of questions in a variety of formats gives students with different learning strengths several opportunities to demonstrate their abilities and knowledge. Some people recall facts easily and do well on short-answer tests. Others are better at expressing themselves in essay writing.
- Exams often need to test a wide range of material, and one kind of question format can't cover it all.
- The instructor wants to test both recognition of key concepts in the material and the recall of information and must use different types of questions to test both.

PRACTICAL PURPOSES

There are also some straightforward reasons for varying question format. These include

- Some kinds of questions are easier for the instructor to write, so they're used along with more complex questions.
- An instructor may have time constraints, which means that at least some of the questions have to be in a short-answer format because they take less time to mark.
- It's more interesting to mark a variety of questions on a large number of test papers. (And it's more interesting for you as a test taker, too.)

STRATEGIES FOR ANSWERING QUESTIONS

How you approach a question depends on what type of question it is.

TRUE/FALSE QUESTIONS

True/false questions are statements that you must identify as accurate or inaccurate based on your knowledge of the subject. Answering such questions correctly is not always just a matter of knowing whether a statement is factually correct. Instructors often use true/false tests to get you to analyze the information given and make judgments based on your careful reading of the questions. Here are some things to watch for.

Questions That Contain Absolutes or Other Qualifiers

Absolutes are statements that offer no alternatives. Words that are absolutes include *always, never, best, worst, none, all, only, everyone, no one,* as in this example:

Students should *never* study immediately before sleep. True or false?

Another type of qualifier is an addition to a basic statement that gives it a different meaning, as in the example here:

Students should allow *very little* time to pass between study and sleep. True or false?

In the first example, you would immediately eliminate True because the statement is an absolute. Very few things in life are absolute, and absolute statements on tests are almost always false. In the second example, the qualifier makes the statement sound reasonable. As you read in Chapter 4, sleep should follow study with little or no interference, so the second statement is True.

Questions That Contain Negatives

Be alert for prefixes to words and words themselves that make the statement mean the opposite of the truth, as in these examples:

> Students should *not* plan to sleep immediately after study.

> Research generally shows that it is *un*wise to sleep immediately after study.

If you recall from Chapter 4 that going to sleep right after studying improves the chances of retention, then making this fact negative—by having the negative word in the first and the negative prefix in the second—makes both statements false.

Questions with Information Designed to Mislead

A question with misleading information in it can confuse the real issue at hand, as in this example:

> Students may *watch television* between sleep and study, but should not *listen to the radio* between sleep and study.

The real issue here is whether or not it is wise to do anything between studying and sleeping. You know from Chapter 4 that it is best to go right to sleep after studying. Therefore, one should not listen to the radio *or* watch television between studying and sleeping, so this statement is false.

Some questions are written to confuse the student by adding false information to an answer that would otherwise be true. For example, "Environmentalists concerned about the impact of global warming cite the greenhouse effect and comprehensive health care as matters demanding government attention." Environmentalists may be interested in the greenhouse effect where global warming is concerned, but health care would not be the concern of that same group. In order for an answer to be true, all the parts of the answer must be true.

MATCHING COLUMNS

The main thing to remember when you are taking a matching column test is to read both columns carefully before matching *anything*. Once you have read both lists all the way through you can start to match the two pieces that belong together. Remember that the correct answers are there for you. It merely remains for you to make good choices among those that seem to match up. Here are some ways of making these good choices:

1. Start with the first item in column A. Search all the way through column B until you locate the best answer. You may see more than one as you work your way down the column, so don't be hasty in making your choice.

2. When you have made a choice from column B, draw a circle around it so that you know it's out of the running for the time being. Don't scratch it out because you may want to take another look at it later if you have doubts about your first choice. If you have scratched it out, you may not be able to see it to reconsider.

3. If you don't find a match for one term, don't waste time searching right away. Leave it blank and come back to it when you have fewer choices available to you.

4. If you find a second match and are unsure of which is the better choice, write the letters of both choices beside the term in column A and return to them later. You will probably find that one of your choices has been taken for another item.

5. Remember that most instructors add one or two extra choices to column B so that you can't work entirely by the process of elimination. Sometimes these extra items are silly and you can eliminate them easily. But sometimes they're tricky because the instructor has chosen a sound-alike or look-alike term to confuse you.

6. When you write the letter of the match in column A, remember to write your letters carefully so that the letter *I* doesn't look like the letter *L*, *G*s like *Q*s, and *M*s like *N*s.

Match the columns below for practice.

Column A	Column B
_____ **1.** annotations	**a.** last-minute, intensive study
_____ **2.** mnemonics	**b.** diagram of key ideas in text
_____ **3.** mapping	**c.** intermittent study
_____ **4.** cramming	**d.** memory losses
_____ **5.** distributed practice	**e.** margin summaries
	f. memory tricks

Note that choices **a** and **c**, and **d** and **f** could easily be mistaken for each other.

Here are the correct answers:

Column A	Column B
_e_ **1.** annotations	**a.** last-minute, intensive study
_f_ **2.** mnemonics	**b.** diagram of key ideas in text
_b_ **3.** mapping	**c.** intermittent study
_a_ **4.** cramming	**d.** memory losses
_c_ **5.** distributed practice	**e.** margin summaries
	f. memory tricks

COMPLETION QUESTIONS

These questions are made up of a stem or partial statement that has to be completed to make sense. Completion questions, along with identification questions, are the hardest of the short answer formats because they rely almost entirely on your recall of information. There are some ways of looking at these questions, though, that may be helpful:

1. Watch for clue words in the *stem* of the question.

Two ways to x-ray text for main ideas are _____ and _____.

The term *x-ray* may trigger your memory of *mapping* and *annotating*.

2. Watch for clues in the *words* in the question.

_____comes from a medical term that means that you sort out the wounded into *three* categories of seriousness. In this book it refers to determining which subjects you should give priority to, which you should spend the most time studying for an upcoming test or tests.

If you know that the prefix for three is *tri*, you may more easily recall that the word you're looking for is *triage*.

3. Watch for *grammatical* clues in the question.

An_____learner learns best by listening.

Of the three types of learners you've read about earlier in this book, only *auditory* can take the article *an*. The terms *visual* and *kinesthetic* would need to be introduced by the article *a*. (A smart teacher, though, won't give you such a clue. She would write "a/an" instead.)

IDENTIFICATIONS

Identifications are words and terms you need to recognize and then be able to define or explain in your own words. Identifications are often names of people, procedures, places, historical locations, or events. On literature tests you may have to identify important characters in a book or play.

This kind of question leaves you very much on your own to retrieve what you remember about the word or term and to express that information clearly. Here's some good advice for answering identification questions:

1. If you don't recall the correct spelling, spell the definition as best you can. Don't leave a space blank because you can't spell the answer. Get at least partial credit.
2. Make your definitions as brief as possible. The instructor is not looking for an essay, just a sense that you are familiar with the term.
3. If you don't remember a name, term, or fact exactly, write what you think you do know about it, like the test taker did in the examples below.

Identifications on a test about twentieth-century women authors:

Betty Friedan: wrote *The Feminine Misteke* (sp?)

The Bloomsbury set: a group of writers in London, I think in
the 1920s

Ayn Rand: wrote about the importance of individualism.

On the following page, try your hand at playing teacher. Write a classroom test on the content of this book so far, using several different types of question formats. A completed sample follows, though your answers will be different.

In Short

Classroom tests may use true/false, matching, completion, and identification questions (in addition to multiple-choice and essay questions). Each kind of question has its own strategies, though reading the question carefully is always key.

CREATE YOUR OWN TEST

Use the form below to write a test on this book.

Mark the following statements as true or false.

1. _____

2. _____

3. _____

4. _____

5. _____

Match the definitions in Column B with the words in Column A below.

Column A   **Column B**

___ 1. _____   a. _____

___ 2. _____   b. _____

___ 3. _____   c. _____

___ 4. _____   d. _____

___ 5. _____   e. _____

___ 6. _____   f. _____

___ 7. _____   g. _____

___ 8. _____   h._____

___ 9. _____   i. _____

___10. _____   j. _____

                                  k. _____

Complete the following sentences.

1. _____

2. _____

3. _____

4. _____

5. _____

Identify the following terms.

1. _____

2. _____

3. _____

4. _____

CREATE YOUR OWN TEST
(Completed sample)

Mark the following statements as true or false.

1. The library is a poor place to study.

2. Studying for long periods of time aids retention.

3. You should never exercise before an exam.

4. Study groups are sometimes good for reviewing information.

5. Family and friends can be helpful in preparing for a test.

Match the definitions in Column B with the words in Column A below.

Column A	Column B
___ **1.** TABE	**a.** marginal summaries
___ **2.** visual modality	**b.** pictorial information
___ **3.** map	**c.** learning by seeing
___ **4.** distractors	**d.** a test for adults
___ **5.** ACT	**e.** a test for public workers
___ **6.** civil service exam	**f.** a classroom test
___ **7.** annotation	**g.** possible answers
___ **8.** graphics	**h.** a diagram of main ideas
___ **9.** stem	**i.** the main idea of the question
___**10.** options	**j.** incorrect answers
	k. a college admission test

Complete the following sentences.

1. It is convenient to write study notes on _____.

2. Sentences that ask you to supply words are called _____.

3. Tests that ask you to identify terms are called _____.

4. Words or phrases that offer no alternatives are called _____.

5. Reading comprehension questions that call for conclusions are _____ questions.

Identify the following terms.

1. mnemonics

2. triage

3. kinesthetic learning

4. cramming

CHAPTER | 12

If you don't know an answer to a test question, don't eliminate your chances by leaving it blank. Make an educated guess. In this chapter, you'll learn how to do just that on many kinds of test questions.

SHOULD YOU GUESS? OFTEN, YES!

You will notice that in all of the test taking strategies noted in the last few chapters, you have read nothing about one of the most obvious approaches to test taking when the answer is not immediately clear: guessing. Most of you have taken a shot at guessing at times on a test, and it is likely that in most cases your guesses were correct and probably were more informed choices than you thought.

You might feel a little guilty about guessing, though. It's a little like saying, "I didn't read that chapter, I just skimmed it." If you got the meaning from the reading, you were reading, regardless of your reading technique. If you get the right answer, you got it right, whether you were guessing or not.

This is not to say, though, that you should guess wildly and without thinking at all. No. You should *choose* to guess and do it in a systematic, purposeful way.

WHEN TO GUESS

You should guess when

- There is no penalty for doing so
- You are absolutely sure you know *nothing* about the question
- You are unsure about a choice between two plausible answers

However, some tests, including the SAT, deduct a quarter of a point for each incorrect answer. You can still guess on these questions, but you should be selective and make educated guesses.

TAKE EDUCATED GUESSES
GUESSING ON MULTIPLE-CHOICE TESTS

As you know, multiple-choice questions usually have four or five options, only one of which is right. Theoretically, each answer gives you a 20–25 percent chance of being correct. If you raise the odds by eliminating one or more of those distractors right away, you are in an even better position to make a good guess. The problem is, what do you do when you have two answers that sound equally correct?

Use the True/False Test

Try submitting the stem and each of the two options you are using to a true/false test.

1. The primary responsibility of the office manager is to
   a. get the CEO's coffee promptly
   b. oversee the general operation of the office
   c. hire and fire other office staff
   d. plan the office Christmas party

After you eliminate **a** and **d** because they are clearly not primary responsibilities, you can look at both of the others in a true/false context.

The *primary* responsibility of the office manager is to over-see the general operation of the office. True or false?

The *primary* responsibility of the office manager is to hire and fire other staff. True or false?

Between these two it seems clear that the truer of the statements is that the manager oversees general operations. While she may indeed participate in hiring decisions, it is unlikely that it is her primary responsibility. Notice that the key word in the stem is *primary*.

This strategy is particularly helpful when you are given options such as *all of the above, none of the above,* or *only 2 and 4 above.*

Go for the Middle

When you are guessing on multiple-choice questions that have numerical options, look for mid-range numbers among your options.

2. In the last ten years, the number of reported incidences of domestic violence has increased by
   a. 22%
   b. 10%
   c. 75%
   d. 5%

Without any other information you might want to choose **a** or **b** simply because they are in the middle of the range provided by all four answers.

In classroom tests, it often seems that the correct answer among multiple-choices is the longest or the one in the middle. (This seems to be less true in standardized tests and civil service tests.)

3. Research indicates that people learn most effectively when they study in
   a. a cram session
   b. two short sessions
   c. several short sessions over a period of time
   d. one long session
   e. groups

If you've been reading this book carefully, you don't have to guess on this question. But if you didn't have a clue, and if this were a classroom test, you might go for answer **c** just because it's longest.

Try Your Best-Guess Strategies First

Choose the middle or the longest option only when you have absolutely no clue as to the right answer and have exhausted more informed approaches. Also, be aware that many test makers know that people have a tendency to guess this way and guard against it by not putting the correct option in the middle or making it the longest one.

GUESSING ON TRUE/FALSE QUESTIONS

On classroom tests, there are more likely to be more true answers than false ones because false answers are harder for the instructor to write. Therefore, if you have to take a guess, choosing True is probably the better bet.

Be careful of tricky wording in true/false questions.

Negatives

Negatives in a statement turn it into its opposite meaning.

4. Dispute over states' rights was not a major cause of the U.S. War Between the States. True or false?

To test the truth of this kind of question, simply take out the negative word and see if the question is true. Negatives in a statement can be confusing because people are not accustomed to reading something when it's in negative terms.

Absolutes

Absolutes qualify a statement to an extreme. You'll recall from Chapter 11 that you should be wary of words like *all, always, solely, never, none, best, worst*. On true/false tests, however, these words can help you because they usually signal that a statement is false.

5. Smoking tobacco has been responsible for all forms of respiratory disease. True or false?

On the basis of the absolute, here the word *all*, you would choose False.

Word Structure

Use anything you know about vocabulary and structure to trigger recognition or recall of information.

> **6.** Bicameral government has two houses in the legislature. True or false?

If you remember that the prefix *bi* means two, then you'd make an educated guess that this statement is true.

GUESSING ON MATCHING COLUMNS

Success at guessing on matching columns depends on how many guesses you have to make. If you are guessing between two choices, the odds are the same as those on true/false—50 percent. If you are guessing at more than two, your odds are lower on each answer. This means that you should begin by reading all of the options. Then begin by matching those you are certain of, thereby reducing the number of difficult matches you have left to guess.

GUESSING ON COMPLETION QUESTIONS

It's hard to guess on questions that require retrieval of information, but some instructors will give partial credit for inexact answers that nevertheless answer the spirit of the question.

> **7.** A _____ economic policy is one in which the government allows the private sector to dominate.

If you couldn't remember *laissez faire*, but did remember what it meant, you could have written *hands off* and might have received partial credit.

Sometimes a guesser is aided by a careless test maker who will give away clues such as the *a/an* advantage. In such a case, if there is the word *an* before the blank, then you can assume that the correct answer starts with a vowel.

> **8.** The group represented a _____ religious faith.

If the test taker were torn between two words, for example, *evangelical* and *Pentecostal*, the *a* would give it away. *Pentecostal* is correct because it is introduced by *a*. Wise test makers, however, cover themselves in these matters by putting *a/an* before such blanks.

On the next page see how well you can figure out the answers to questions based on guessing strategies alone.

IN SHORT

If you don't know the answer to a question, make an educated guess. Turn multiple-choice questions into true/false questions to test each possible answer. Watch out for the use of negatives in true/false statements and be wary of absolutes, such as *none, never, all, always,* and *best.* Even if you don't remember the complete answer for a short-answer question, write down what you do know because you may receive partial credit.

TEST YOUR GUESS-ABILITY

Without any information to guide you on these questions, see what educated guesses you can make. Then take a look at the answer sheet to see how well you did.

Multiple-choice questions

1. When not responding directly to a fire, a firefighter's main responsibility is
   a. maintaining the firefighting apparatus
   b. upholding the image of the department in the community
   c. delegating responsibilities in the firehouse
   d. keeping in good physical condition

2. Dr. Martin Luther King led the March on Washington in
   a. 1960
   b. 1968
   c. 1972
   d. 1985

3. A reader's ability to comprehend what he or she is reading depends upon
   a. intelligence
   b. reading speed
   c. prior knowledge or familiarity with the content
   d. phonics
   e. whole language

True/false questions

_____ 1.　　　Preservation of the union was not a primary considera-tion in the American Civil War.
_____ 2.　　　All greenhouse gases are harmful to humans.
_____ 3.　　　Recycling does not materially affect environmental quality.
_____ 4.　　　Geology is the study of the earth and its properties.
_____5.　　　Gandhi's call for non-violent resistance failed to unite his country against colonial rule.

Completions

1.　The botanical term for plant reproduction is _____.
2.　　A plant that goes to seed and dies at the end of the growing season is called an _____.

TEST YOUR GUESS-ABILITY

(Answer sheet)

Multiple-choice questions

1. When not responding directly to a fire, a firefighter's main responsibility is
   a. maintaining the firefighting apparatus
   b. upholding the image of the department in the community
   c. delegating responsibilities in the firehouse
   d. keeping in good physical condition

2. Dr. Martin Luther King led the March on Washington in
   a. 1960
   b. 1968
   c. 1972
   d. 1985

3. A reader's ability to comprehend what he or she is reading depends upon
   a. intelligence
   b. reading speed
   c. prior knowledge or familiarity with the content
   d. phonics
   e. whole language

True/false questions

___F___ 1. Preservation of the union was not a primary consideration in the American Civil War.

___F___ 2. All greenhouse gases are harmful to humans.

___F___ 3. Recycling does not materially affect environmental quality.

___T___ 4. Geology is the study of the earth and its properties.

___F___ 5. Gandhi's call for non-violent resistance failed to unite his country against colonial rule.

Completions

1. The botanical term for plant reproduction is propagate.

2. A plant that goes to seed and dies at the end of the growing season is called an annual.

CHAPTER | 13

Here's advice for pacing yourself when you take a test to increase your chances for getting all the points you can get in the time you are allowed. You'll learn what to do when you're starting the test, how to proceed through the middle, and what to do with any time you have left at the end.

MANAGING YOUR TIME DURING THE SHORT-ANSWER TEST

In Chapter 8, you went through the general management of a test day: before, during, and after your test. In Chapters 9–12 you met the kinds of multiple-choice and other questions you might encounter on those tests and learned how you might make educated guesses on questions of which you are unsure.

Now that you know how to approach short-answer questions and even take educated guesses, let's look at how to deal with those questions under testing conditions. It goes without saying that it's very important for you to plan and pace your approach to tests carefully. There are few things more disappointing than losing control of a test after long and sometimes painful preparation!

BEFORE YOU START
PREVIEW THE TEST

There should be no surprises when you get to any section of the test. It's like taking a trip through the woods: it's helpful to know where you are going and what you will encounter along the way.

There are two reasons that you should preview a test very carefully before you start working:

- You want to find out where rough spots are on the test, so you can prepare to spend more time on those sections.
- You want to be familiar with the content of the whole test so that you have a good overall picture of what topics are stressed and know the formats for all of the sections of the test. Then, as you go back and work through the test, you're revisiting familiar ground.

ARE SECTIONS TIMED?

See if each section of the test has been assigned a time frame.

Vocabulary:	20 minutes
Reading Comprehension:	40 minutes
Math computation:	30 minutes
Verbal Expression:	30 minutes

If you are allowed to write in the test book, circle those times so you are well aware of how long you have for each section.

HOW LONG IS THE TEST?

Count or take note of the number of pages in the test. The reason for this will be clear later.

READ OR LISTEN TO DIRECTIONS CAREFULLY

If allowed, always underline or circle key words in the instructions that cue you to what the question requires. Follow the directions to the letter. This will be covered in more detail later.

GETTING STARTED
ASSIGN TIMES TO SECTIONS

If there is no time frame already allowed for each section of the test, quickly figure out how much time you think you will need to allow for each section. Base your assessment on your best guess of what sections will be easiest for you. For example, if you feel more comfortable in math, allow for less time there than for the sections that will be tougher for you, like reading. If you're allowed to write in the test book, quickly jot down a time allowance for each section in the margin at the start of each section.

For example, a civil service test might include the following in a one-hour test. Based merely on your own comfort level, how much time would you allot to each of the following sections for that hour?

Vocabulary	8 questions	____minutes
Comprehension	3 paragraphs with 10 questions	____minutes
Math	22 questions	____minutes
Language mechanics	10 questions	____minutes
Grammar	10 questions	____minutes
Spelling	10 questions	____minutes

MATCH TIME TO TEST POINTS

Note how much each section of a test counts in terms of total test points. It is foolish to waste time fretting over short-answer questions that count less than an essay that's worth much more. If you've sketched out in your mind how much time you want to spend on each section, you will know when you're beginning to waste time. Plan to spend longer on the sections that count more. If you haven't finished one section and it is time to go on to another that carries more points, do so.

DON'T LINGER TOO LONG ON ANY ONE QUESTION

Answer the questions in a section or on the whole test that you know the answers to for certain right away. If you are unsure about a question, put a dot in the margin next to that question so you can find it easily when you want to come back to it later. Don't linger too long over questions you can't answer right away. You may find that other questions on the test will steer you to the best choices for questions that at first seem difficult to you.

NOTE SPECIAL DIRECTIONS

Take special note of directions involving choice or selection. For example, if in the directions for a section of 15 examples, it says, "Write definitions for 10 of the following," don't write definitions for all 15! You won't get any bonus points for doing all 15, nor will the instructor search around the test paper for your *best* 10. You'll only waste precious time.

HOW TO AVOID PANIC

There are times when you may feel absolutely panicked in the middle of a test. If you are feeling shaky because you see too many unfamiliar questions on the test, are running out of time, or have just run out of energy for a while, here are some techniques for keeping yourself from coming unglued:

1. Stop writing for a minute or two and relax.
2. Sit back in your chair. Let your arms and head drop down and breathe slowly and deeply for a few seconds.
3. Try to empty your mind of all its worries. Visualize the end of the test.
4. Stretch your arms, hands, neck, and shoulders.
5. Take off your sweater. Put on your sweater.
6. Blow your nose, or pop a mint in your mouth.
7. Return to the test with a get-tough attitude.

Sometimes you have to make a triage decision about the test. For instance, decide where on the test you can make the most points in the time you have left. Concentrate on doing the very best you can in those areas. You'll feel better when you have regained control over yourself and over the test.

WHEN YOU HAVE TIME LEFT

If you've followed the suggestions in these chapters and conscientiously maintained control over the timing, you may find that you have time left over after you have finished the test. Do not throw down your pen and sigh with relief that the test is over—at least not yet! Remember, this is not a race. You don't win by being first over the finish line. Resist the temptation to leave right away.

Here are some suggestions for making the best possible use of any time left over.

DON'T LEAVE ANYTHING OUT

Make sure you don't have any unfinished business:

- Count the pages of the test book again. Double-check that you didn't skip a page because two pages stuck together or you accidentally turned two pages at the same time. Now is the time to do any work you missed this way. Imagine losing credit for a whole section on the test because you didn't see it and didn't do it! It happens.
- Go back and look for any questions you were uncertain about. This is why it's wise to put a dot in the margin next to tough questions. When you don't have much time at the end of a test, you want to make it as easy as possible to find those questions you were unsure about earlier.
- Look at the problem questions with a fresh pair of eyes. They may not seem as difficult or confusing as they did the first time you saw them. They may be clearer in light of other questions you've now answered.
- If you have unanswered questions left, decide whether it's best to leave them blank or take an educated guess in hopes of getting some credit. Remember the tips for smart guessing in Chapter 12.

DOUBLE-CHECK YOUR ANSWERS

After you've made sure you've answered (or decided not to answer) all the questions, check for accuracy and completeness in your answers.

- Make sure each answer you've chosen is entered on the correct spot on the answer sheet and is legibly written. Second only to the anger at having missed whole sections accidentally is the irritation of having put correct answers in the wrong places on the answer sheets.
- Make sure your numbers and letters are clear and carefully written. You don't want to have your 4 look like a 9, or an *M* be read for an *N*.

- If you change an answer, make sure you change it completely. Write the new answer down before you erase the old answer.
- If you change an answer, be doubly sure of its accuracy now. Generally speaking, your first choices are the best choices on short-answer questions. If you change your mind, it should be for some specific reason, not just a gut feeling or intuition. Check essays for grammar and punctuation. Make sure there's nothing you want to add to the text (see Chapter 16).

Give yourself some practice in planning and pacing a test by using the following page to make a time schedule for one of the sample tests in Chapters 17–19. A completed sample follows.

IN SHORT

You can manage your time during short-answer tests by previewing the test before you begin. Look to see if the sections have time limits and write them down. Estimate how long it will take you to complete each section and note any special directions about how points are calculated. If you have extra time left at the end of the test, review your work and complete any questions you left blank during your first time through the test.

TIME SCHEDULE FOR _____
TEST IN CHAPTER _____

Preview the tests in Chapter 17–19 and choose one. Write a time schedule for that test.

Section	Minutes
_____	_____
_____	_____
_____	_____
_____	_____
_____	_____
_____	_____
_____	_____

TIME SCHEDULE FOR <u>STANDARDIZED</u> TEST IN CHAPTER <u>18</u>
(Completed sample)

Section	Minutes
Vocabulary	10
Spelling	5
Language Mechanics	5
Language Expression	10
Math	10
Reading Comprehension	20

CHAPTER | 14

In this chapter, you'll learn how to get ready to take an essay or extended-answer test, with strategies for predicting question topics in advance.

PREPARING FOR ESSAY QUESTIONS

Essay and extended-answer questions require that you not only remember or recall facts, but that you also organize and present these facts in a written summary. Unlike short-answer questions, these longer answers are usually considered to be *subjective* because they ask you to give your own interpretation to the information.

Essays are usually at least a paragraph in length and organized into a structure that includes an introduction, development of one or more ideas, and a conclusion. An extended-answer question is similar to a short-answer completion question, except that it requires more than just a word or phrase. It may ask for one or more complete sentences, a list, definitions, or steps in a process.

WHY ARE ESSAYS SO POPULAR ON EXAMS?

Essay and extended-answer questions are used on exams because they allow an instructor to test for—and a student to demonstrate—different kinds of skills and knowledge.

ADVANTAGES

Essay and extended-answer questions allow
- The instructor to ask for proof of a wider knowledge of the subject than can be asked for in a short-answer question
- The student to demonstrate some breadth of knowledge beyond the range of the question itself
- An opportunity for those students whose strengths are in writing or communications to show their talents
- The instructor to gauge the writing skills of the student as well as the student's knowledge of the subject

DISADVANTAGES

The disadvantages of essay and extended-answer questions are as follows:
- They are time-consuming to take.
- They are time-consuming to grade.
- They are graded partly on the instructor's judgment of your writing skill rather than strictly on the knowledge you show in answering the actual question.
- They may penalize students whose language and writing skills are less well developed.

WHAT DO YOU STUDY?

If you know that a large percentage of a test is going to be comprised of essay and extended-answer questions, you have to prepare for the test in specific ways.

CLASS NOTES

Do a thorough review of all your class notes. Start with these notes because most instructors have specific matters and viewpoints that they repeat fairly often through the semester. List specific ideas that were raised in lectures, but are not in the text.

Borrow and photocopy a set of notes from a classmate. Compare them with your own notes. Add anything that you may have missed in your own notes. You may want to write notes from other sources in a contrasting ink so that you remember where that information came from.

HANDOUTS

Next, do a thorough review of all handout materials—articles copied from newspapers, periodicals, or journals, for example—and make notes in the margins of any themes or ideas that echo those of the class notes.

> **Where's the Emphasis?**
> Some instructors organize a course around their own lectures and use the textbook and handouts only as supplementary materials. Others use the book as the main source of the course and supplement it with lectures and handouts. Decide whether your course is book-centered or instructor-centered so you have some idea about what the instructor is likely to emphasize on the test.

TEXTBOOKS

Read the highlighted text and margin notes you made in your textbooks. List separately any ideas that reinforce or contrast the ideas in the class notes and handouts. Read the titles, subtitles, advance organizers (margin notes or headings that alert you to what is in the text), chapter summaries, and introductions.

Look for sections at the end of chapters that say things like *Questions to Think About*. More than one instructor has drawn test questions directly from a book's lists of questions.

HOW TO PREPARE
ANALYZE YOUR PREVIOUS TEST EXPERIENCES

Look at other essay tests you have taken and been graded on. Recall the kinds of errors you may have made on the tests. And make note of instructors' comments about your essays, such as:

- Doesn't answer the question
- Too vague
- Be careful of punctuation

FIND OUT ABOUT PAST TESTS

Get as much information as you can about previous tests in this course by this instructor.

- Ask the instructor what areas will be covered by the essay questions. Listen carefully to the answers you get.
- Ask students who have taken the course before to tell you about the instructor's tests. Listen to the *buzz* about the tests in this course. Most instructors have a reputation for being interested in specific things. Word gets around.
- Do not fall for offers of previous tests that will tell you what questions will be on the test. Most instructors don't give the same test every year. It does help to know what *kind* of questions that instructor may favor, though.
- Find out whether the instructor or someone else grades the exams. You may have more leeway with an instructor who already knows your work from the class, and you could pitch your essays to those areas you know the instructor emphasized in class. If a teaching assistant grades the papers, you may have to be more specific in the language that you use and the points you raise that may have come from class discussions or personal conversations with the instructor.

BRAINSTORM WITH YOUR CLASSMATES

Group study is good for essay test preparation because groups lend themselves more to the give and take of discussion than to facts learned for short-answer recall. You can benefit from the interpretations of other minds.

Talk through concepts, philosophies, themes in literature or other possible essay topics with your study group. Share the work of making up sample essays for an exam. Have each person in the study group contribute one possible essay question based on your conversations in the group. Then have everyone in the group write answers for these practice essays. Compare your answers.

STUDY STRATEGIES

Play instructor. Once you have assembled all the information that seems to be important for essay questions on your test, make up imaginary questions on the main ideas you have noticed in the course. Think what questions you would ask if you were the instructor.

BE FAMILIAR WITH TERMS USED IN ESSAY QUESTIONS

One way to anticipate essay questions is to know the kinds of things you may be asked to write about. The table below shows a list of the most common key words used in essay questions.

Key Words	Meaning	Example
Trace	Describe the process or development of an idea, practice, or social/political phenomenon.	Trace the development of entitlement programs in the U.S. since the New Deal.
Describe	Make a detailed, sequential picture of a series of events.	Describe the main events leading to the outbreak of the War Between the States in 1861.
Discuss	Analyze in considerable detail all aspects related to an event, a social or political trend, an idea, or point of view.	Discuss the color symbolism in the novel *The Great Gatsby*.
Evaluate	Make a judgment about specific facts or circumstances. (Sometimes the word you see in questions like this is *criticize.*)	Evaluate the effort to reinstate prayer in the public schools.
Explain	Clarify and give reasons for the ideas in the material.	Explain the need for regulations in the securities industry.
Defend	Give one side of an argument and offer reasons for your opinion.	Defend the practice of diplomatic immunity.
Summarize	Condense a large amount of information into a shorter format.	Summarize the arguments supporting legalization of marijuana.

There are other terms that are used for extended-answer tests. This second table shows some of the less common terms.

Key Word	Meaning	Example
Enumerate	Present information in a sequential manner.	Enumerate the stages of bereavement.
List	Make an itemized series of names or terms.	List three major civil rights initiatives in the 1960s.
Give examples	Note instances illustrating the main idea.	Give four examples of 20th-century artistic movements.
Identify	Define or characterize names, terms, places, or events	Identify three branches of the federal government.

MAKE CHARTS

You might make charts similar to the study notes described in Chapter 4. They consist of the question on one half of the page and the answer on the other. The questions can be phrased in several ways that are typical of essay exams.

Here's an example of a chart for an essay question on global warming:

Global Warming	
Causes	Destruction of rain forests Ozone depletion
Effects	Melting of the ice caps Changes in climate patterns Disruption of food production
Solutions	Decrease dependence on fossil fuels Ban the use of CFCs Preserve the rainforest

Other charts could show

- **Comparisons/contrasts.** Compare the Red Scares of the 1920s with the Communist Witch-hunts of the 1950s.
- **Pros and cons** (or benefits/risks, advantages/disadvantages). Describe the arguments for and against a balanced budget amendment in Congress.
- **Theories/theorists, writers/works.** Evaluate the contributions of feminist writers in the Women's Liberation movement of the 1970s.

The benefit of the chart format is that you can fold the paper lengthwise and quiz yourself with the questions on one side, and then check your answers on the other.

MAKE NOTE CARDS

Note cards can be a great help when you're learning factual information for short-answer tests—and they can be just as helpful when studying for essays. In fact, you may be able to use some of your factual cards to provide the details you need for a good essay answer.

Note cards for preparing for essays can be organized as follows:

- Sort note cards into piles that pertain to specific topics
- On the face of a clean card, write a sample essay question for each pile of cards.
- Put the question card and all the cards that pertain to that question together. Review the cards often over a period of time before the test. Your constant review of the subject matter will help you respond to any question you might be asked on that topic.
- Make note cards that contain the main facts you want to include on specific essays. This will reduce a large number of facts to a small number of notes that you can carry with you to review when you have any time to spare throughout the day.

MAKE OUTLINES

Imagine some essay questions you might be asked on your test. Then write outlines of your essay answers. Outlining streamlines the information you want to remember to include in an essay. Here is an example:

Define global warming. Describe the proposed risks of global warming. Suggest possible solutions to the problem of global warming.

   I. What is global warming?
  II. Risks of global warming
      A. Melting ice caps
      B. Changes in climate patterns
      C. Disrupted food production
 III. Solutions to global warming
      A. Preserve the rain forests
      B. Reduce dependence on fossil fuels
      C. Reduce uses of CFCs

MAP THE MAIN IDEAS

If you are a highly visual learner, you may want to prepare your practice essays by making a diagram or map of the main points you need to remember. Like the x-ray strategy described in Chapter 4, mapping shows just the skeleton of the essay, but it's easy to retrieve and then flesh out when you're actually taking the test.

On the following page, make study plans to prepare for essay questions you think might be included on a test based on this book.

IN SHORT

Essays and extended-answer questions are popular on classroom exams because they allow the instructor to test the student's breadth of knowledge and writing skills at the same time. You can prepare for these types of questions by studying your class notes, handouts, and textbooks. Get together with other students to form a study group and make note cards to carry with you for daily review.

STUDY STRATEGIES

Practice preparing for an essay test by using the study strategies explained in this chapter. Then compare your study strategies with those on the completed sample.

Make a comparison chart on the benefits and drawbacks of essay questions on tests.

Outline the principal kinds of multiple-choice questions included in this book.

Map the two main question formats with examples of each.

Make note cards for the steps needed to avoid panic on a test.

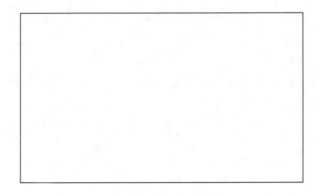

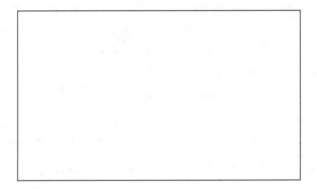

STUDY STRATEGIES

(Completed sample)

Make a comparison chart on the benefits and drawbacks of essay questions on tests.

Benefits	Drawbacks
wider knowledge	time-consuming to take
show verbal strength	time-consuming to grade
test writing skills	use judgment
show more knowledge	penalize poor skills

Outline the principal kinds of multiple-choice questions included in this book.

I. Recognition
    A. Facts
    B. Reading comprehension
II. Recall
    A. Math and graphic aids
    B. Common-sense and reasoning

Map the two main question formats with examples of each.

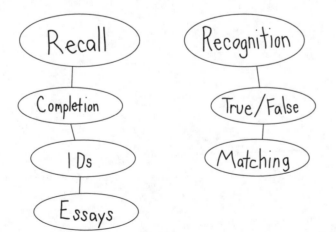

Make note cards for the steps needed to avoid panic on a test.

Stop writing :
   Breathe deeply
Visualize success

Be physical :
   Stretch
   Take off / put on sweater
Eat a mint or chew gum
   Get tough!

CHAPTER | 15

You've done your studying and know your facts. This chapter will show you how to express what you know clearly and convincingly in essay form.

TAKING AN ESSAY TEST

Is writing essay answers on tests different from writing essays for an English class? Yes and no. There are some similarities. For instance, you need to be clear and accurate as well as grammatically correct, and you must communicate what you know to someone else. The difference in writing essays for exams is that you must write within a time limit, and you have to organize your thoughts without the benefit of a textbook or notes.

HOW TO GET STARTED
READ ALL THE QUESTIONS FIRST

It is particularly important to read all the questions first because sometimes questions are related to each other. You don't want to waste all your good points on one question when you may be able to use them on two or more questions.

You also want to be alerted to the subjects of the test so that you can allot extra time to think about questions you hadn't anticipated.

UNDERSTAND EACH QUESTION COMPLETELY

Just answer the question

Don't write everything you know about a subject when you are only asked for specific information. Keep to the question. It is very tempting to put in lots of facts if you happen to know a good deal about the topic. The instructor, however, does not want to spend time reading extra material and will want to read only what's specifically required by the question.

There are few things more annoying than getting an exam returned with comments like, "Good essay, but you've written on the wrong topic" or "You didn't answer the question that was asked."

It's vital that you know exactly what the instructor is asking.

- **Underline the key words or phrases** in the questions that describe what is being asked for.
- **Don't just repeat** what's been written when you are asked to explain.
- **Don't just define** when you are asked to discuss. This is particularly important when questions themselves are long and complicated.

HOW TO WRITE A GOOD ESSAY

Let's take things step by step, beginning with a sample question.

Define and give examples of business franchises. Discuss the risks and benefits of these kinds of businesses. Describe the factors that will determine the future of franchising.

1. Confine yourself to the question. Limit your discussion just to what is required by the key words or phrases of the question.
2. Make a time-frame for the test. When you first look at the test, do

what you do in any test: figure out how much time you will have to complete each question. Note how much each question is worth and write next to the question in the margin how much time you will spend on the question.

The general rule is to spend one half of the time allotted to a question to planning the answer—by outline or map—and one half to the actual writing of the answer. For example:

Question #1, 20 minutes total—10 minutes to plan, 10 minutes to write.

3. Make a map or outline of every answer. As you read each question, jot down all the facts you can remember about the subject right away. Write them in the margin of the test book. After you have assessed how much you will say and how long you will take to say it, be sure to get that information down in a form you can follow. Outline or map the information you want to use to answer each question so that you have a visual image of all the facts or opinions you want to include in your answer.

> **Partial Credit Is Better than None at All**
> If you run out of time for writing your answer but you have all the points you want to make in your outline or map, the instructor may give you some credit, since it is obvious you know more than you were able to explain in the essay.

STRUCTURING YOUR ESSAY
THE THESIS STATEMENT

Start your essay by restating the question as your thesis statement. A thesis statement is a preview of the main ideas you will develop in the essay. Get in as many of the key words from the question in your thesis statement as you can. Here's an example:

Franchises, defined as businesses like Carvel or McDonald's that are authorized to offer a product or service owned by a parent company, offer both risks and rewards to the business owner.

CHOOSE A FORMAT

Decide upon how you will structure the answer to each question. You can simply restate your map or outline in paragraph form. Or you can organize it by one of the patterns that work well in essay tests: pros and cons, comparisons or contrasts, and opinions with reasons.

Each segment of your outline or map should be a separate paragraph that is introduced by a topic sentence. A topic sentence is a summary of the details that follow in the paragraph. Here's an example of a flow chart style map:

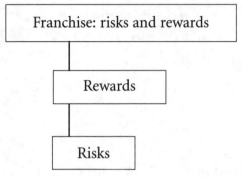

Then proceed to translate that map into an essay answer by writing your thesis statement. Follow that with two paragraphs, focusing each of them on one of the elements of your map.

> Franchises, defined as businesses like Carvel or McDonald's that are authorized to offer a product or service owned by a parent company, offer both risks and benefits to the business owner. (**thesis statement**)

> First, let's look at the three main benefits of franchising. (**topic sentence**) The first of these is name recognition, which is helpful in marketing a known product. Secondly, a franchise offers a uniform and widely known product. Finally, there are low operating costs made possible by the parent companies.

> On the other hand, there are risks to running franchise businesses. (**topic sentence**) Franchise businesses do not have the independence to alter the products or services to suit individual markets. Franchisees are also at the mercy of the corporate health of the parent company. If the parent company is doing poorly because of mismanagement in one part of the country, all franchises are compromised.

WRITING THE ESSAY

Make your writing style suit the occasion:

- **Be concise and precise.** Keep your sentences short and simple and don't pad your answer by repeating the same idea in different ways. Always be as *specific* as possible in making the points you want to make.

- **Use enumeration.** Introduce the points you want to make by using labeling words like, "There are *three* major advantages to franchise businesses. The *first advantage* of these is name recognition."

- **Use signaling words.** Signal words guide your reader through your essay. These include such words and phrases as:

To begin with	However
Next	Consequently
Therefore	In conclusion

- **Avoid nonstandard forms or trendy idioms.** Don't use nonstandard forms in test essay writing.

  Jane Jacobs tells it like it is when she talks about life in the 'hood'.

  Not everyone (including perhaps the person marking your test) will know what the expression *life in the hood* means. A better way of writing it is:

  Jane Jacobs tells some hard truths about life in urban neighborhoods.

- **Refer to authors and people of note by their last names.**

  Jacobs [not Jane] believes that urban planning has ignored the importance of neighborhood life in the development of the city.

- **Keep your handwriting as legible as possible.** It may be difficult to make your words and sentences clear when you are rushing to finish on time. Have pity on the person who must read a stack of papers, each with a different way of writing. A neat and easy-to-read paragraph or essay is welcomed—and often rewarded—by the instructor.

- **Leave space between essays.** Skip a line or two so that you have some blank space should you want to add information that comes to mind later.

IF WHAT YOU STUDIED ISN'T ON THE TEST

You have a great answer, but no question to go with it! Don't beat yourself up for making wrong assumptions. Don't be hard on yourself for believing your classmate. (*Somebody told me Professor Jones always asks a question on the development of the trade union movement.*) If it happens to you, here are a couple of suggestions:

- Try to match up some of the information you predicted with what has been asked. You may not remember all the important information about the franchising business, but some of the information you prepared about unions may have some relevance to the franchising question.
- Put all the information you can recall about the subject at the beginning of your essay. Do as much as you can with what little you remember. Take special care that what information you have is well presented. You may get points for presentation if not for content.

AT THE END OF THE TEST

Read your essay answers carefully for accuracy in spelling, grammar, and punctuation. Make sure you have capitals and periods at the beginnings and ends of sentences. Write over corrected words carefully.

Compare your answers against your outlines or maps to make sure you have picked up every point you planned to make on the test. If you see that you left out something important, write it below the question or, if you didn't leave extra room on your paper, then in the margin.

Look at your answers critically. Pretend you are the instructor who is reading the essays. What would you think of your work?

Be sure your name is on every test book. Many essay tests require several test books (usually called *blue books* though they come in many colors). Booklets can get separated during the grading process, so be sure each one you use has your name and that all books are fitted together (second and third books inside the first) before you hand the whole batch in to the instructor or proctor.

IF YOU FEEL YOU'VE BEEN GRADED UNFAIRLY

In spite of all your preparation, you may get an exam back that carries a disappointing grade. If that happens, it is natural for you to be upset. The first person you want to blame, of course, is the instructor. It's easy to jump to the conclusion that he or she made mistakes in grading your paper. But here's what you should do instead:

- **Read over your paper carefully.** It is possible that the instructor accidentally skipped one of your essays, or added the points incorrectly. Check out these possibilities first.

- **Read over your paper critically.** If you don't find some obvious reason for the low grade, see how it sounds to you now. Did you show what you knew in the most organized, clearest, most concise, most accurate way possible? Read the instructor's comments. Try to understand the instructor's criticisms.

- **Confront your teacher cordially.** If you are still convinced that you deserve a better grade, make an appointment to see the instructor. Approach the instructor with an attitude of inquiry. Explain that you want to know how to prepare more successfully for the next test. Bring your test to your interview and bring written questions about the test to discuss. Really listen to what the instructor says about the test. Learn from your mistakes before the next exam.

On the following page try out your essay-writing ability by making a time plan and writing the answers for a short essay exam.

In Short

You can express your knowledge clearly and convincingly in an essay test by organizing your answer before you begin to write it out. Spend half the allotted time planning your answer by outlining or mapping and half your time writing the answer itself. Read all of the questions before you answer any of them and remember to write legibly!

PRACTICING ESSAY ANSWERS

In 45 minutes, answer each of the following questions in a well-developed paragraph. Before you begin, decide and note how long you plan to spend on each question based on its point value. Use the space below to outline or map your answers. Write the essay answers on separate sheets of paper.

1. Explain the need for a diet and exercise plan before taking a major test. Give examples of good diet and exercise habits. (30 points) _____min.

2. Identify three learning modalities, or styles, and tell how a student would use each modality to aid in test preparation. (30 points) _____min.

3. Discuss the similarities and differences between studying for a civil service or standardized test and studying for a classroom test. (40 points) _____min.

PRACTICING ESSAY ANSWERS
(Completed sample)

1. In order to do your best on a test, it is important to pay attention to the diet and exercise your body needs to do its best. **(Thesis statement)** Good health that comes from nutritional foods and regular exercise helps you to concentrate, combat fatigue, and avoid illness during the stress of studying over long periods of time.

   As you prepare to take a major test, be careful to maintain a good, well-balanced diet. **(Topic sentence)** Stay away from salty snacks or processed foods that contain extra salt. Limit your intake of coffee and soda. Try not to order out prepared foods very often. Keep regular mealtimes instead of grazing during the day.

   During test preparation, your body also needs regular exercise to offset long hours spent sitting at your desk. **(Topic sentence)** Be sure to do some form of aerobic exercise at least three times a week. Take walks to rest from study several times a day. Make an effort to participate in vigorous exercise through team sports or individual activities such as swimming, jogging, or biking.

2. No two people learn exactly alike. Everyone has a unique learning style. There are three specific styles by which people learn. **(Thesis statement)** These are the visual, the auditory, and the kinesthetic or tactile modalities.

   People who learn best visually like to see what they need to learn. **(Topic sentence)** Visual learners should color-code important information. They should map or outline information from their textbooks to get a strong visual cue for memorizing. They should pay special attention to pictures, maps, charts, and other visual references while they read.

   People who learn best by listening are auditory learners. **(Topic sentence)** They should read aloud to themselves or others. They should tape-record notes and play them back during study sessions. Auditory learners also benefit from working with a study group in which they can hear the views of other students.

Kinesthetic or tactile learners learn by interacting physically with the text. (**Topic sentence**) They should take lots of notes and underline or highlight text as they read. Some kinesthetic learners are helped by copying or re-copying class notes or notes from the textbook.

3. There are both similarities and differences in the methods for studying for occasional tests such as the GED or a civil service test and those needed to prepare for a classroom test. (**Thesis statement**)

There are two important ways in which preparation for a standardized or civil service test is similar to preparing for a class test. (**Topic sentence**) First, you need a systematic and organized study plan. Secondly, you need to develop the learning strategies that will allow you to study effectively.

Students must also realize, however, that there are distinct differences between preparing for classroom, civil service, and standardized tests. (**Topic sentence**) Classroom tests contain a wider variety of questions. Standardized and civil service tests are usually all multiple-choice. Class tests are designed to reflect the specific instructor's interests and expertise. Civil service and standardized tests do not offer the opportunity to anticipate the questions the instructor is likely to include on the test.

CHAPTER | 16

It's not just what you say, it's also how you say it. In this chapter, you'll learn how to improve the basic writing skills you need to have to score well on essay tests.

WRITING BASICS FOR THE ESSAY TEST

The content of your essay answer is certainly important, but so is the language you use to convey that information. That's why this entire chapter is devoted to how to make your extended-answer questions well-organized, clear, concise, and accurate.

HOW TO WRITE IN AN ORGANIZED WAY

Outline or map your essay first. These visual strategies for organizing information before you start to write are very helpful. They're the quickest way for you to get your ideas down on paper. When you first open your test, you should spend *one half* of whatever time you decide to spend on the question in making a map or outline of what you have to say.

Below are some organizing diagrams that can be used to set up your essay before you start writing.

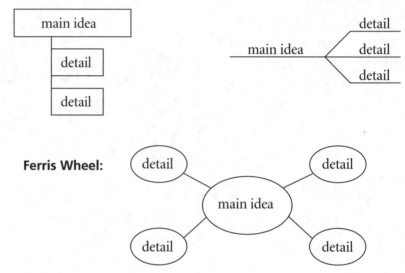

Flow chart:

main idea

detail

detail

Ladder:

main idea

detail

detail

detail

Ferris Wheel:

detail

detail

main idea

detail

detail

EXPRESSING YOURSELF CLEARLY
USE THE SPECIFIC VOCABULARY OF YOUR SUBJECT

It's a good idea to be prepared with the words (properly spelled!) that pertain to the subject of the essay question. As you study, write down the words you think are important to the subject on note cards.

For example, in a course in economics you should know the following words:

annuities	margins
deficits	discount rates
	equities

For a course in English literature you would want to know terms such as:

imagery	irony
exposition	symbolism
narrative	genre

You should also be prepared to cite specific names of characters, authors, acts, laws, theories, and important people in your subject areas.

BEWARE OF EASILY CONFUSED WORDS AND TERMS

Here are some terms used in essay writing that are often misused because they sound or look alike.

Term	Meaning	Example
illusion	a misleading impression	He had no illusions about her feelings.
allusion	a reference to a commonly known source	The Biblical allusion was good.
advise	to give counsel; a verb	I advise you to study hard.
advice	a recommendation; a noun	Dad gave me good advice.
principle	a basic truth or law	The principle of truth in advertising was challenged by the tobacco companies.
principal	the head of a school	The new principal addressed the sixth grade assembly.
affect	to influence; a verb	Her injury did not affect her performance.
effect	the result of an action; a noun	Her childhood trauma had an enormous effect on her life.
farther	a greater distance	He can skate farther than his sister.
further	in addition	There will be no further discussion until the attorney arrives.
quote	to cite someone else's language; a verb	He liked to quote his father's wise advice.
quotation	the citation of someone's work	He included numerous quotations of scientific studies in his monograph.
lose	to mislay something; a verb	He didn't want to lose the election.
loose	unattached; an adjective	He was considered a loose cannon that couldn't be controlled by Congress.

BE AWARE OF THE DIFFERENT FLAVORS OF WORDS

Many words that people use in writing have both denotations and connotations. This means that words have meanings or feelings—*connotations*—that go beyond their dictionary definitions—their *denotations*. Thus, words have different *flavors*, depending on their use in a sentence.

The words *fat, obese, chubby,* and *plump* all suggest that someone is overweight. However, we associate *chubbiness* and *plumpness* with appealing images of babies and small children, while words like *obese* and *fat* call up mental pictures of unattractive heavy grownups.

If you were describing a particular human behavior, for instance, you might think about the difference in the images suggested by the word *aggressive* as opposed to the flavor of the word *assertive*. Which word best expresses the attitude you observed?

WRITING CONCISELY
KEEP SENTENCE STRUCTURE SIMPLE

The basic subject-verb-object sentence structure is always safe to use in an essay test. It will be boring for your instructor to read, however, if you don't vary the sentence structure somewhat.

Pare Down Long Clauses to Words and Phrases

Less is often better. For example, you could write:

> The hero, who was dashing and romantic in the early part of the book, turned out to be the villain in the end.

However, the following sentence is cleaner and stronger:

> The romantic hero was later revealed to be the villain.

Use Strong Verbs

Get in the habit of using meaningful verbs. For example, look at this sentence:

> The social worker is charged with supervising and writing reports on thirty clients a week.

More meaningful verbs would make the sentence look like this:

> The social worker supervises and reports on thirty clients a week.

Always use active voice instead of passive whenever possible. Here is the passive:

> Firefighters have been instructed by their superiors to open all vents in the room before removing the flammable substance.

Here is the active voice:

> Supervisors have instructed firefighters to open all vents before removing the flammable substance.

Keep the Language Clean and Clear

Get yourself accustomed to writing in a straightforward way. You can be expressive and convincing without the help of unnecessary adverbs, adjectives, and extra clauses.

Leave Out Unneeded Words or Phrases

The italicized words in the next two sentences aren't essential; they just take up space—and take extra time to read:

> *It has been said that* we all bear responsibility for the actions of our government. *It would seem certain that* the new Congress will bring about badly needed reforms.

Don't Repeat Yourself

Be careful not to say the same thing twice in two different ways. For example, in the two sentences below, one set of italicized words should be taken out to avoid repetition.

> He had no idea how to solve the *troublesome* problem *that was bothering him. At this point in time* he feels that action should be taken *now*.

Don't Try to Make It Sound Fancy

Very informal language has no place in essay test answers. And neither does overly formal or elaborate language. Don't use a long, complicated word or expression when a simple one will do equally well. For instance:

> The facilitator in the learning station will offer positive reinforcement to the learner.

That sentence is better written as the following:

> The instructor in the classroom will give the student a pat on the back.

AVOIDING LANGUAGE MISTAKES

One of the challenges of writing essay answers for a test is that they have to be written within a time limit. When you feel pressured by the clock, it's easy to be sloppy in the so-called mechanics of writing—the spelling, grammar, and usage skills—that are essential in a good essay answer. And during a test, you don't have access to the computer's spell checker or grammar checker!

There's no room here for a detailed review of spelling and grammar skills—just examples of the kinds of errors to avoid because they *show*. These are the mistakes that are so ugly they call attention to themselves. They stand out and take the spotlight away from the good ideas you may have expressed.

DON'T COMMIT ANY MAJOR USAGE ERRORS

Here are the top ten errors on the *zit parade*—words that mess up the pretty face of your writing.

ERROR	RULE	EXAMPLE
Don't confuse *its* and *it's*.	*It's* is a contraction meaning *it is.*	*It's* a long journey.
	Its is a possessive pronoun.	Virtue is *its* own reward.
Don't confuse *fewer* with *less* and *amount* with *number*.	*Fewer* and *number* are used things you can specifically count.	There are *fewer* calories in soda. We gave to a large *number* of charities.
	Amount and *less* are used with things you can't specifically count.	We have *less* time to relax. He had a large *amount* of cash.
Don't use *of* for *have*.	*Should of* and *would of* are incorrect.	I *should have* gone alone. I *would have* eaten earlier.
Don't say *use to* and *suppose to*.	*Used to* and *supposed to* are correct.	I *used to* work at Macy's. He was *supposed to* go to the game.
Don't say *the reason why is because*	You are saying the same thing twice. Rephrase the sentence.	I said Judy was in camp *because* I thought it was true.
Don't confuse *their*, *there*, and *they're*.	*There* is an adverb telling where.	Put it over *there*.
	They're is a contraction for *they are.*	*They're* going to the movies.
	Their is a possessive pronoun.	They wore *their* coats.

ERROR	RULE	EXAMPLE
Never say *is when* or *is where*.	These are unnecessarily wordy phrases.	Mapping *is* a diagram of ideas in writing. (*not* Mapping is when you diagram your ideas in writing.)
Don't confuse subjects and verbs.	Make subjects and verbs agree.	*John*, along with his sister Jane, *has* a long commute to school.
Rewrite sentence to make pronouns match their nouns.	Don't use a plural pronoun when you are trying to be gender neutral.	Rewrite Everyone go to *their* seats as They will go to *their* own seats.
Don't confuse *to*, *two*, and *too*.	*To* is a preposition. *Too* means also.	She is going *to* school. Her brother is going *too*.
	Two is a number.	They will take *two* buses.

WATCH FOR MAJOR GRAMMATICAL ERRORS

Avoid the big grammar mistakes that can drive instructors to early retirement.

- Underline (or italicize when you're using a computer) titles of books, magazines, films, plays, musical compositions, and newspapers: In an article in the *New York Times* . . . .
- Put quotes around titles of poems, short stories, and titles of magazine articles: In the short story, "Paul's Case" . . . .
- Capitalize proper nouns—names, places, languages, historical epochs, official course titles, organizations, political parties, and titles: Jefferson is considered to be the father of the Democratic Party. Make sure your capitals look like capitals!
- Use periods, question marks, or exclamation points at the ends of sentences.
- Don't use apostrophes for plurals: He had two exams (not exam's) on the same day.
- Don't use quotation marks for emphasis: He wanted to go to "gym," not the park, after lunch. This sentence is not correct; there is no reason to use quotation marks here.

DON'T MAKE ANY MAJOR SPELLING ERRORS

Sound out words in your mind if you are not sure how to spell them. Remember that long vowels inside words are usually followed by single consonants: *sofa, total.* Short vowels inside words are usually followed by double consonants: *dribble, scissors.*

Give yourself auditory listening clues when you learn words. Say *Wednes-day* or *lis-ten* or *bus-i-ness* to yourself when you spell so that you remember to add the letters you don't hear.

Look at each part of the word. See if there is a root, prefix, or suffix that will always be spelled the same way. For example, in *uninhabitable, un, in,* and *able* are always spelled the same way. What is left is *habit,* a self-contained word that is not difficult to spell.

Check your command of the English language by correcting the sentences on the next page.

IN SHORT

You can present your ideas in a well-organized and concise way while writing an answer to an essay question. Avoid making glaring language mistakes by reviewing basic grammar and spelling rules before the test. Keep your sentence structure simple but varied.

TEST YOUR LANGUAGE SMARTS

Rewrite the sentences below to correct errors in mechanics or usage.

1. Their are many reasons why you should outline your essay before you write.

   _____

   _____

2. The speaker used excellent quotes that had a great affect on his audience.

   _____

   _____

3. They should of gone too they're counselor's before leaving school that day.

   _____

   _____

4. According to the New York Times less students are enrolling in ROTC programs than in the 1980s.

   _____

   _____

5. Economically disadvantaged persons have difficulty remitting their revenue enhancements.

   _____

   _____

6. A single parent often has only their common sense to rely on.

_____

_____

7. The hard working employee was very diligent.

_____

_____

8. I was told by the IRS that my "refund" would be late.

_____

_____

9. In my considered opinion "The Great Gatsby", a novel by F. Scott Fitzgerald, is the most significant book to be written in this century.

_____

_____

10. FDR took a lot of heat with his lend lease act prior two our getting involved with WW2.

_____

_____

TEST YOUR LANGUAGE SMARTS

(Completed sample)

1. Their are many reasons why you should outline your essay
   before you write.

   There are many reasons for outlining your essays before you write.

2. The speaker used excellent quotes that had a great affect on
   his audience.

   *The speaker used excellent quotations that had a great effect on
   his audience.*

3. They should of gone too they're counselor's before leaving
   school that day.

   *They should have gone to their counselors before leaving school that
   day.*

4. According to the New York Times less students are enrolling in
   ROTC programs than in the 1980s.

   *According to the <u>New York Times</u>, fewer students are enrolling in
   ROTC programs than in the 1980s.*

5. Economically disadvantaged persons have difficulty remitting
   their revenue enhancements.

   Poor people have trouble paying their taxes.

6. A single parent often has only their common sense to rely on.

   Single parents often must rely only on their common sense.

7. The hard working employee was very diligent.

   He was a hard-working employee.

8. I was told by the IRS that my "refund" would be late.

   The IRS notified me that my refund would be late.

9. In my considered opinion "The Great Gatsby", a novel by F. Scott Fitzgerald, is the most significant book to be written in this century.

I believe that Fitzgerald's <u>The Great Gatsby</u> is this century's best novel.

10. FDR took a lot of heat with his lend lease act prior two our getting involved with WW2.

Many were critical of the Lend Lease Act proposed by President Roosevelt before our entry into World War II.

CHAPTER 17

In this chapter, you will find a sample test modeled on those given across the country to applicants for civil service jobs in police, fire, sanitation, correction, and clerical positions. Use the strategies you've learned so far to answer the questions.

TEST YOURSELF: A PRACTICE CIVIL SERVICE TEST

This sample test is designed to take approximately one hour. If you are working with the book for 20 minutes a day, you may want to break up this test so that you complete one-third of it at a time and finish it in three days. It might be wise, however, to break from your regular 20-minute-a-day routine and take a full hour so that you can complete the test in one sitting. This will give you better practice in pacing your work and sustaining the effort it takes to take a test all at once.

Remember to take a few minutes to preview the entire test, so you know what's in store for you before you start answering questions.

PART I: VERBAL EXPRESSION

1. Which of the following reports expresses a traffic incident most clearly and accurately?

   a. A red light was run on April 19, at 11:34 p.m. at the intersection of Maple Avenue and Grove Street. The officers at the scene were Officers Harrow and Ortiz. The aforementioned officers arrested Henry Clark of 112 Aspen Street and took him into custody. Mr. Clark refused to take a test for DWI. He was taken to the station house at 12:00 a.m.

   b. Officers Harrow and Ortiz arrested Henry Jones of Aspen Street for running a red light at Maple Avenue and Grove Street at 11:34 p.m. on April 19. Mr. Jones refused to take a test for DWI and was taken to police headquarters at 12:00 a.m.

   c. After running a red light and refusing to take a DWI test, police officers Harrow and Ortiz arrested Henry Jones of Aspen Street. It was 11:34 on April 19th that they made the arrest and took him to the station house at midnight that night.

   d. Henry Jones refused a DWI test, so Officers Harrow and Ortiz escorted him to police headquarters at 12:00 a.m. when he ran a red light at the corner of Maple Avenue and Grove Street. This was on April 19th at 11:34 p.m. Mr. Jones lives at 112 Aspen Street.

2. Which of the following reports expresses a job-related incident by a sanitation worker most clearly and accurately?

   a. January 23, I was making my usual stops on Center Street when I saw a steep driveway with a blue Camry sliding down. It was very icy. I couldn't stop in time and the car hit my right front fender. The driver of the car was Mrs. O'Brien of 233 Center Street. She was not hurt and neither was I or my truck. But the car had a lot of damage. I called the police and my supervisor at the sanitation garage.

   b. On January 23 I was on my route on Center Street when a car slid out of a driveway and hit my truck. The car was driven by Mrs. O'Brien who was not hurt. Her car, a blue Camry, had a lot of damage. She lives at 233 Center Street and her driveway was very icy. I was not hurt either, so I called the police and my supervisor to report the incident.

c. On January 23, a blue Camry car driven by Mrs. O'Brien of 233 Center Street slid on an icy driveway at that address and struck my truck on the right side. Neither Mrs. O'Brien nor I were hurt in the accident, but her car sustained considerable damage. Following the accident, I called the police and my supervisor at the sanitation garage.

d. I was not hurt, but sliding down an icy driveway at 233 Center Avenue, Mrs. O'Brien who lived there slammed into my truck which was making its usual route. She hit my truck on the right hand side and her blue Camry sustained a great deal of damage. Mrs. O'Brien wasn't hurt either. I reported the accident to the police and to my supervisor.

In questions 3–5, find the word that means the same or almost the same as the underlined word.

3. The <u>alleged</u> perpetrator denied he was at the scene of the crime.
  a. suspected
  b. guilty
  c. lying
  d. remorseful

4. The <u>conscientious</u> sanitation worker always replaced the covers on the trash cans.
  a. careless
  b. caring
  c. careful
  d. contentious

5. Capt. O'Mara was <u>designated</u> to represent the department during Fire Prevention Week.
  a. insulted
  b. chosen
  c. hired
  d. trained

In questions 6–8, choose the sentence that is punctuated correctly.

6. a. Though he was officially off duty Sanitation Worker Mendez helped to clear the trash from the vacant lot.
  b. Though he was officially "off duty", sanitation worker Mendez helped to clear the trash from the vacant lot.
  c. Though he was officially off duty, sanitation worker Mendez helped to clear the trash from the vacant lot?
  d. Though he was officially off duty, sanitation worker Mendez helped to clear the trash from the vacant lot.

7. a. Officer Takamura shouted "Stop! You are under arrest."
  b. Officer Takamura shouted, "Stop! You are under arrest."
  c. Officer Takamura shouted ! "Stop, You are under arrest."
  d. Officer Takamura shouted "Stop, you are under arrest."

8. a. The Firefighters responded to a call at 467 e. Fulton st.
  b. The firefighters responded to a call to 467 E Fulton st.
  c. The firefighters responded to a call to 467 E Fulton Str.
  d. The firefighters responded to a call at 467 E. Fulton St.

For questions 9–10, choose the correct spelling of each word.

9. a. cashier
  b. casheir
  c. cashere
  d. casheer

10. a. interveiw
  b. inervew
  c. interview
  d. intervue

PART II: READING COMPREHENSION

Answer the questions in this section solely on the basis of the passages that precede them.

At 1:30 a.m., while parked at 917 Crescent, Police Officers Lin and Lawton were asked to respond to a call from Tucker's Tavern at 714 Clarinda. At 1:42 a.m., when the officers arrived, they found paramedics attempting to revive 18-year-old Brent Morrow, who lay unconscious on the floor. A patron of the tavern, Edward Pickens, stated that at around 12:10 a.m., Mr. Morrow's two companions had playfully challenged Mr. Morrow to "chug" a pint of whiskey and that Mr. Morrow had done so in approximately 15 minutes. Mr. Pickens thought the two should be arrested. Mr. Morrow's companions, Jeremy Roland and Casey Edwards, denied Mr. Pickens' statement. The bartender, Raymond Evans, stated he had not served Mr. Morrow and that Tucker's Tavern does not sell whiskey by the pint. At 1:50 a.m. paramedics took Mr. Morrow to University Hospital where he remains unconscious. No arrests were made. An investigation is pending.

11. Which of the following persons most likely called police to Tucker's Tavern?
    a. Raymond Evans
    b. Brent Morrow
    c. Jeremy Roland
    d. Edward Pickens

12. What was the main reason Brent Morrow was removed from Tucker's Tavern?
    a. He was drunk.
    b. He was under-age.
    c. He was ill.
    d. He was a university student.

13. What is the most likely reason Brent Morrow's companions challenged him to "chug" a pint of whiskey?

a. They thought it would be fun.

b. They wanted him to get sick.

c. They thought it was time he "grew up."

d. They were trying to get even with him.

14. At about what time did Brent Morrow finish "chugging" the pint of whiskey?

a. 12:25 a.m.

b. 1:30 a.m.

c. 1:42 a.m.

d. 1:50 a.m.

Firefighters know that the dangers of motor vehicle fires are too often overlooked. In the United States, one out of five fires involves motor vehicles, resulting each year in 600 deaths, 2,600 civilian injuries, and 1,200 injuries to firefighters. The reason for so many injuries and fatalities is that a vehicle can generate heat of up to 1,500°F. (The boiling point of water is 212°F, and the cooking temperature for most foods is 500°F.)

Because of the intense heat generated in a vehicle fire, parts of the car or truck may burst, causing debris to shoot great distances and turning bumpers, tire rims, drive shafts, axles, and even engine parts into lethal shrapnel. Gas tanks may rupture and spray highly flammable fuel. In addition, hazardous materials such as battery acid, even without burning, can cause serious injury.

Vehicle fires can also produce toxic gases. Carbon monoxide, which is produced during a fire, is an odorless and colorless gas but in high concentrations is deadly. Firefighters must wear self-contained breathing devices and full protective fire-resistant gear when attempting to extinguish a vehicle fire.

15. One reason that firefighters wear self-contained breathing devices is to protect themselves against

a. flying car parts

b. intense heat

c. flammable fuels

d. carbon monoxide

16. The passage suggests that most injuries in motor vehicle fires are caused by
   a. battery acid
   b. odorless gases
   c. extremely high temperatures
   d. firefighters' mistakes

17. The main focus of this passage is
   a. how firefighters protect themselves against motor vehicle fires
   b. the dangers of motor vehicle fires
   c. the amount of heat generated in motor vehicle fires
   d. the dangers of odorless gases in motor vehicle fires

18. The cooking temperature for food (500°F) is most likely included in the passage to show the reader
   a. how hot motor vehicle fires really are
   b. at what point water boils
   c. why motor vehicle fires produce toxic gases
   d. why one out of five fires involves a motor vehicle

19. One reason that firefighters must be aware of the possibility of carbon monoxide in motor vehicle fires is because carbon monoxide
   a. is highly concentrated
   b. cannot be seen or smelled
   c. cannot be protected against
   d. can shoot great distances into the air

   While preserving evidence is not the firefighter's main priority, certain steps can be taken, while fighting a fire, to maintain site integrity and maximize efforts of investigators.

   Try to determine the point of origin from wind direction or the way the fire spread. Take notes, mentally and on paper, of suspicious people or vehicles. Use ribbon or other practical material to flag potential evidence, such as tracks near the suspected point of origin and items such as matches, bottles, rags, cigarette butts, lighters, paper, or exposed wires. Keep other personnel away from these areas unless doing so would hamper firefighting efforts.

After flagging the evidence, notify the commanding officer as soon as possible. If evidence must be removed, handle it carefully to maintain fingerprint integrity.

Once the fire is declared under control, create a map of the scene, indicating the point of origin and areas where evidence is or was located. Compose an inventory of any evidence that was removed. Record any other useful information, such as conversations with witnesses, names, and descriptions. Before leaving, share your findings with the lead investigator.

Remember, safety is the main priority during the fighting of a fire. But by keeping an alert eye for clues, you can also contribute to an efficient investigation into its cause.

20. According to the passage, which of the following is the main responsibility of a firefighter?
    a. to maintain the integrity of the site
    b. to flag evidence and keep an inventory of it
    c. to operate in a safe manner
    d. to provide support for investigators

21. The passage suggests that the first step the firefighter should take after evidence is flagged is to
    a. bring it to the attention of the officer in command
    b. create a map of the scene
    c. see how it relates to the point of origin
    d. indicate its location to investigators

22. Which of the following would a firefighter NOT necessarily do after the fire is brought under control?
    a. create an inventory
    b. carefully remove the evidence from the scene
    c. log witness descriptions
    d. record flagged evidence areas

23. Which of the following best expresses the subject of this passage?
   a. how to aid investigation into the cause of a fire
   b. how to maintain safety while investigating a fire
   c. the importance of flagging evidence during the fighting of a fire
   d. what to do with flagged evidence of the cause of a fire

24. According to the passage, fire personnel should be instructed to avoid areas where evidence is found
   a. only after the fire has been brought under control
   b. only if the fire can also be fought effectively
   c. only if the evidence points directly to the cause of the fire
   d. only until the commanding officer is informed

During the next ten months, all bus operators with two or more years of service will be required to have completed twenty hours of refresher training on one of the Vehicle Maneuvering Training Buses. These buses are actually simulators that reproduce lifelike driving experiences. The simulators are linked by computer to a driving course. The driver sits in one room in a life-size replica of a real bus while a two-foot bus attached to the computer moves around the course in the next room, simulating the driving experience.

Instructors who have used this new technology report that trainees develop skills more quickly than with traditional training methods. In refresher training, this new system reinforces defensive driving skills and safe driving habits. Drivers can also check their reaction times and hand-eye coordination.

The city expects to save money with the simulators because the new system reduces the amount of training time in an actual bus, saving on parts, fuel, and other operating expenses.

25. All bus operators with two or more years of service are required to do which of the following?
   a. receive training in defensive driving and operating a computer
   b. complete ten months of refresher driver training
   c. train new drivers on how to operate a simulator
   d. complete twenty hours of training on a simulator

26. The main purpose of the refresher training course on the simulator is to
    a. make sure that all bus operators are maintaining proper driving habits
    b. give experienced bus operators an opportunity to learn new driving techniques
    c. help all bus operators to develop hand-eye coordination
    d. reduce the city's operating budget

27. The bulletin announcing the refresher training course is posted on April 1. If you are a bus operator with two or more years of service, this means you will be required to finish your training by the following
    a. January 31
    b. February 28
    c. March 31
    d. December 31

PART III: COMMON SENSE AND JUDGMENT QUESTIONS

Use good judgment and common sense to answer the questions that follow.

28. The fire department has replaced its wooden ladders with aluminum ladders. Which of the following is NOT a sensible reason for this change?
    a. Wooden ladders are harder to repair and keep clean.
    b. Wooden ladders are less expensive than aluminum ladders.
    c. Wooden ladders are heavier than aluminum ladders.
    d. Wooden ladders catch on fire more readily than aluminum ladders.

29. For the past two months stereo shops all over the city have been hit by burglars in the early morning hours. Sergeant Adams tells Officer Bryant that he should carefully watch the stores in his area that specialize in stereo equipment. Which one of the following situations should Officer Bryant investigate?
  a. a truck with its motor running backed up to the rear door of the House of Stereos at 2 a.m.
  b. an elderly couple window shopping at the House of Stereos at 10 p.m.
  c. a delivery van marked "House of Stereos" parked in the rear of the store at 11:30 p.m.
  d. two teenaged boys intently examining a stereo system in the window of House of Stereos at midnight

30. One rainy afternoon you are picking up trash in a residential neighborhood. You have just gotten back into your truck to drive to the next pick-up point, when you see an elderly woman about half a block away, walking toward you, struggling to carry a small bag of trash. What should you do?
  a. drive on, as regulations state all trash should be set out before pickup time
  b. wait for the woman to bring the trash to you, but thank her for her efforts
  c. drive on, as it is extremely important not to be late driving a pick-up route
  d. get out of the truck, walk to the woman, and take the trash from her

31. You are a bus driver on your regular route. You pull up to the bus stop and open your doors to let passengers on. A man with a very large dog on a leash tries to board the bus, despite the sign saying "No Animals Allowed." The dog is barking and struggling to get away from the bus. Which of the following is the best action for you to take?
  a. overlook the rules this one time in the interest of good public relations
  b. ask someone in the crowd to help the man get his dog onto the bus
  c. exit the bus and help the man get the dog on board
  d. tell the man he cannot bring pets onto the bus and refuse to allow him to board

PART IV: GRAPHIC PRESENTATION

Questions 32–36 are based on the schedule for headway times shown below. Headway times are the intervals between two successive buses moving in the same direction on the same route.

HEADWAY TIMES IN MINUTES

Time	Weekdays	Saturdays	Sundays
12:00 Midnight to 5:00 am	30	30	30
5:00 am to 6:30 am	15	30	30
6:30 am to 9:30 am	5	15	30
9:30 am to 2:30 pm	12	15	30
2:30 pm to 4:00 pm	10	15	30
4:00 pm to 7:00 pm	5	15	30
7:00 pm to 12:00 Midnight	15	15	30

Note: The Saturday schedule will be in effect on Presidents Day. The Sunday schedule will be in effect on all other holidays.

32. A bus leaves a stop at 2:45 p.m. on a Tuesday. If a woman arrives at the same stop at 2:50 p.m., how long will she wait for another bus to arrive?
   a. 3 minutes
   b. 5 minutes
   c. 7 minutes
   d. 12 minutes

33. What is the difference between the headway times at 7:00 a.m. on a Thursday and 7:00 a.m. on a Sunday?
   a. 10 minutes
   b. 15 minutes
   c. 25 minutes
   d. 30 minutes

34. A man knows that on weekdays there is a 9:30 a.m. bus at the stop nearest his home. One Friday, however, he cannot get to that stop until 9:55 a.m. When can he expect the to board a bus?

   a. 10:00 a.m.

   b. 10:03 a.m.

   c. 10:06 a.m.

   d. 10:10 a.m.

35. If a woman arrives at a bus stop at 5:00 p.m. on Presidents Day, which is a Monday, what is the longest period of time she should have to wait before a bus arrives?

   a. 5 minutes

   b. 12 minutes

   c. 15 minutes

   d. 30 minutes

Answer questions 36 and 37 on the basis of the following information.

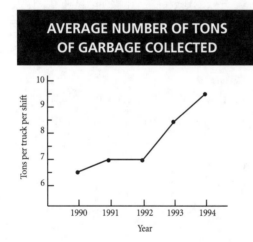

36. According to the graph, what was the number of tons of garbage collected per shift per truck in 1990?

   a. $6\frac{1}{2}$

   b. $7\frac{1}{2}$

   c. $8\frac{1}{2}$

   d. $9\frac{1}{2}$

37. According to the graph, which period of time showed the smallest increase in tons per truck per shift collected?

   a. 1990–1991
   b. 1991–1992
   c. 1992–1993
   d. 1993–1994

Answer questions 38 and 39 by referring to the following graph, which shows fire fatalities statewide for certain ages.

1994 Fire Fatalities Statewide, ages 1 through 64

RACE / GENDER	1-4	5-9	10-14	15-19	20-24	25-34	35-44	45-54	55-64	Totals
White Male	7	1	0	2	2	9	8	7	4	40
White Female	7	1	0	1	0	2	3	1	6	21
Non-White Male	5	3	2	0	0	5	8	3	7	33
Non-White Female	3	3	0	0	2	3	3	2	1	17
Totals	22	8	2	3	4	19	22	13	18	111

Note: For the purposes of this study, persons under 20 years of age are classified as children. Persons 20 years of age and older are classified as adults.

38. According to the graph, the greatest number of fatalities among children aged 1–14 occurred in which group?

   a. white males
   b. non-white males
   c. white females
   d. non-white females

39. If the trend shown on the graph continues in future years, which of the following statements is accurate?

   a. Fewer white males than white females will die.
   b. Fewer white females over age 20 than white females under 20 will die.
   c. More adults than children will die.
   d. More non-white persons than white persons will die.

PART V: MATH APPLICATIONS

40. When a sprinkler system is installed in a home that is under construction, the system costs about 1.5% of the total building cost. The cost of the same system installed after the home is built is about 4% of the total building cost. How much would a homeowner save by installing a sprinkler system in a $150,000 home while the home is still under construction?

a. $600

b. $2,250

c. $3,750

d. $6,000

41. If one gallon of water weighs 8.35 pounds, a 25-gallon container of water would most nearly weigh

a. 173 pounds

b. 200 pounds

c. 209 pounds

d. 215 pounds

42. A safety box has three layers of metal, each with a different width. If one layer is $\frac{1}{8}$ inch thick, a second layer is $\frac{1}{6}$ inch thick, and the total thickness is $\frac{3}{4}$ inch thick, what is the width of the third layer?

a. $\frac{5}{12}$

b. $\frac{11}{24}$

c. $\frac{7}{18}$

d. $\frac{1}{2}$

43. Studies have shown that automatic sprinkler systems save about $5,700 in damages per fire in stores and offices. If a particular community has on average 14 store and office fires every year, about how much money is saved each year if these building have sprinkler systems?

a. $28,500

b. $77,800

c. $79,800

d. $87,800

197

44. If a man weighs 168 pounds, what is the approximate weight of that man in kilograms? (1 kilogram = about 2.2 pounds)

a. 76

b. 77

c. 149

d. 150

45. Officer Hesalroad has responded to the scene of a robbery. On the officer's arrival, the victim, Ms. Margaret Olsen, tells the officer that the following items were taken from her by a man who threatened her with a knife:

- 1 gold watch, valued at $240
- 2 rings, each valued at $150
- 1 ring, valued at $70
- $95 cash

Officer Hesalroad is preparing her report on the robbery. Which one of the following is the total value of the cash and property Ms. Olsen reported stolen?

a. $545

b. $555

c. $705

d. $785

46. Last year 220 city residents were cited for violating a local ordinance against open burning. Of those residents, 60% were fined for the violation. How many residents who violated the ordinance were not fined?

a. 36

b. 55

c. 88

d. 132

47. How many feet of tape will a police officer need to tie off a crime scene that is 34 feet long and 20 feet wide?

a. 56

b. 88

c. 108

d. 480

48. About how many liters of liquid will a 50-gallon container hold?
(1 liter = 1.06 quarts)
   a. 53
   b. 106
   c. 206
   d. 212

49. What is the approximate total weight of four people who weigh 152 pounds, 168 pounds, 182 pounds, and 201 pounds?
   a. 690 pounds
   b. 700 pounds
   c. 710 pounds
   d. 750 pounds

50. If a compartment on the back of a recycling truck is 10 feet long, 6 feet wide, and 4 feet high, what is its volume in cubic feet?
(Volume = Length x Width x Height)
   a. 20
   b. 64
   c. 210
   d. 240

Now check your answers with the *Civil Service Test Answers and Explanations* that follow. Note which kinds of questions you missed. Plan to spend some time reviewing those areas in which your performance was weak.

CIVIL SERVICE TEST ANSWERS AND EXPLANATIONS

Part I: Verbal Expression

1. **b.** This is the most concise answer that contains the most information.
2. **c.** This answer contains the most information in an organized format.
3. **a.** *Alleged* means *suspected.*
4. **c.** *Conscientious* means *careful.*
5. **b.** *Designated* means *chosen.*
6. **d.** An introductory clause is followed by a comma.
7. **b.** There is a comma before a quotation.
8. **d.** *Firefighters* is not capitalized; the abbreviations for street and direction need periods.
9. **a.** *Cashier*
10. **c.** *Interview*

Part II: Reading Comprehension

11. **d.** The passage states that Mr. Pickens thought Mr. Morrow's companions *should be arrested.* Mr. Morrow himself is unconscious. Mr. Evans and Mr. Roland would probably be afraid of being blamed for Mr. Morrow's condition.
12. **c.** Mr. Morrow chugged a pint of whiskey in 15 minutes and is comatose.
13. **a.** The passage says that Mr. Morrow's friends' actions were *playful.*
14. **a.** According to Mr. Pickens, Mr. Morrow began to chug the whiskey at 12:10 and did so in about 15 minutes.
15. **d.** The discussion of carbon monoxide in the last paragraph serves to demonstrate why firefighters should wear breathing apparatus.
16. **c.** The dangers outlined in the first and second paragraphs of the passage are all caused by extreme heat.
17. **b.** The other choices are mentioned in the passage but are not the main idea.
18. **a.** The cooking temperature is given to show the difference of 1,000 degrees of heat between a motor vehicle fire and cooking.

19. b. The last paragraph states that *carbon monoxide . . . is odorless and colorless.*

20. c. See the next to last sentence of the passage.

21. a. See the third paragraph.

22. b. The fourth paragraph gives the steps to take after the fire is brought under control, and removal of evidence is not one of them.

23. a. The first sentence states that while fighting a fire, firefighters can take steps to *maximize efforts of investigators.* Virtually all of the passage deals with those steps. Do not confuse the "subject" of the passage with the firefighter's "main responsibility" (option **b**). Options **c** and **d** are only details relating to the main idea.

24. b. The second paragraph states that personnel shall be kept away from flagged evidence, *unless doing so would hamper firefighting efforts.*

25. d. The first two sentences of the passage state that bus operators must have 20 hours of training on a simulator.

26. a. The second sentence in the second paragraph states that the simulator reinforces safe driving habits. Although choices **b**, **c**, and **d** are possible benefits of the program, these are not the main purpose of the refresher course.

27. a. The first line of the passage states that drivers must complete 20 hours of refresher training during the next ten months, which would be the end of the following January.

Part III: Common Sense and Judgment

28. b. The lower cost is an advantage of wooden ladders over aluminum. The other statements are negative statements regarding wooden ladders.

29. a. A truck with the motor running backed up to the rear door of a closed business at 2 a.m. is suspicious. Delivery vans owned by businesses are commonly parked on store property after hours (answer **c**). Window shoppers, whether elderly (**b**) or teenaged (**d**), aren't as likely to be burglars as the scene detailed in answer **a**.

30. d. It would be courteous and good for public relations to help the woman, especially since it will take very little time. The other choices would be unnecessarily rude.

31. d. Since the dog is struggling to get away from the bus and is probably frightened, it would not be safe to allow this animal on board even if transit rules allowed uncrated animals aboard buses.

Part IV: Graphic Presentation

32. b. On weekdays between 2:30 p.m. and 4:00 p.m., buses come every 10 minutes. The woman arrived at the stop 5 minutes after one bus left, so she will only have to wait another 5 minutes.

33. c. On weekdays between 6:30 a.m. and 9:30 a.m., buses leave every 5 minutes; on Sundays, they leave every 30 minutes. The difference is 25 minutes.

34. c. On weekdays between 9:30 a.m. and 2:30 p.m., buses come every 12 minutes. If there is a bus at 9:30, there will also be buses at 9:42, 9:54, and 10:06. If the man cannot get to the stop until 9:55, the next bus will be at 10:06.

35. c. On Presidents Day, the Saturday schedule is in effect; between 4:00 p.m. and 7:00 p.m., buses arrive every 15 minutes.

36. a. The point on the graph for 1990 is closest to $6\frac{1}{2}$.

37. b. In both 1991 and 1992, the amount of garbage collected per truck per shift was 7 tons.

38. b. Ten non-white males died. The next highest number is eight.

39. c. In 1994, 76 adults died, compared with 35 children.

Part V: Math Applications

40. c. First, you must subtract the percentage of the installation cost during construction (1.5%) from the percentage of the installation cost after construction (4%). To do this, begin by converting the percentages into decimals: 4% is 0.04; 1.5% is 0.015. Now subtract: 0.04 − 0.015 = 0.025. This is the percentage of the total cost that the homeowner will save. Multiply this by the total cost of the home to find the dollar amount: 0.025 x $150,000 = $3,750.

41. c. To solve the problem, take the weight of one gallon of water (8.35) and multiply it by the number of gallons (25): 8.35 x 25 = 208.7. Now round to the nearest unit, which is 209.

42. b. To solve the problem, you must first find the common denominator, in this instance, 24. Then the fractions must be converted: $\frac{1}{8} = \frac{3}{24}$; $\frac{1}{6} = \frac{4}{24}$; $\frac{3}{4} = \frac{18}{24}$. Add the values for first and second layers together: $\frac{3}{24} + \frac{4}{24} = \frac{7}{24}$, and then subtract the sum from the total thickness ($\frac{18}{24}$): $\frac{18}{24} - \frac{7}{24} = \frac{11}{24}$.

43. c. To solve this problem, multiply the amount saved per fire, $5,700, by the average number of fires: 5,700 x 14 = 79,800.

44. a. To solve this problem, divide the number of pounds (168) by the number of kilograms in a pound (2.2) to get 76.36. Now round to the nearest unit, which is 76.

45. c. The two rings valued at $150 have a total value of $300, but remember that there is another ring valued at only $70.

46. c. If 60% of the residents were fined, 40% were not fined. Forty percent of 220 is 88.

47. c. There are two sides 34 feet long and two sides 20 feet long. Using the formula P = 2L + 2W will solve this problem. Therefore, you should multiply 34 times 2 and 20 times 2 and add the results: 68 + 40 = 108.

48. d. The answer to this question lies in knowing that there are four quarts to a gallon. There are, therefore, 200 quarts in a 50-gallon container. Multiply 200 by 1.06 quarts per liter to get 212 liters.

49. b. Add all four weights for a total of 703. 703 rounded to the nearest ten is 700.

50. d. This is a multiplication problem using the formula given: 10 x 6 x 4 = 240.

How Well Did I Do on the Practice Civil Service Test? A Self Analysis

I answered ___/10 questions correctly on the *Verbal Expression* section.

I answered ___/16 questions correctly on the *Reading Comprehension* section.

I answered ___/4 questions correctly on the *Common Sense and Judgment* section.

I answered ___/8 questions correctly on the *Graphic Presentation* section.

I answered ___/11 questions correctly on the *Math Applications* section.

I got the most correct answers on the _____ section(s).

I think I did well on these sections because

I got the fewest correct answers on the _____ section(s).

I think I did not do as well in these areas because

In order to do better in these areas, I need to:

_____ review my basic skills in reading, math or vocabulary

_____ read questions more carefully

_____ choose my answers more carefully

_____ work more quickly

_____ work more slowly

Other_____

CHAPTER | 18

In this chapter, you'll practice taking a test modeled on standardized tests such as the GED or TABE. Use the strategies here that you've learned for answering multiple-choice questions.

TEST YOURSELF: A PRACTICE STANDARDIZED TEST

This sample test is designed to take approximately one hour. As with the practice civil service test, the best idea is for you to complete the whole exam in one sitting, though you can break it up so that you complete one-third of the test at a time for 20 minutes a day for three days.

Remember to take a few minutes to preview the entire test, so you know what's in store for you before you start answering questions.

PART I: VOCABULARY

Choose the word that means the same or nearly the same as the underlined word.

1. A <u>gregarious</u> person
   a. fearful
   b. sociable
   c. comical
   d. generous

2. An <u>obsolete</u> attitude
   a. modern
   b. hostile
   c. outdated
   d. welcoming

3. An <u>innocuous</u> statement
   a. harmless
   b. hateful
   c. scripted
   d. public

Choose the word or phrase that most nearly means the opposite of the underlined word.

4. To show <u>antipathy</u> for
   a. friendship
   b. ill-feeling
   c. concern
   d. disdain

5. An <u>arrogant</u> manner is
   a. courtly
   b. angry
   c. annoying
   d. humble

6. <u>Impulsive</u> actions are
    a. spur of the moment
    b. cautious
    c. joyous
    d. fast

Choose the word that best completes each of the following sentences.

7. The _____ smells coming from the kitchen reminded her that she hadn't eaten all day.
    a. bitter
    b. tantalizing
    c. unpleasant
    d. sickening

8. He wrote under a _____ since he didn't want anyone to know his identity.
    a. disability
    b. pseudonym
    c. tree
    d. mask

9. Because he wished to be anonymous, the family was never to know the name of their _____.
    a. lawyer
    b. judge
    c. mortician
    d. benefactor

10. Despite her disability, the girl never let her blindness be a(n) _____ to her success.
    a. asset
    b. hindrance
    c. encouragement
    d. scapegoat

PART II: SPELLING

Choose the word that is spelled correctly and best completes each sentence below.

11. The officer's handwriting was _____.
    a. illegible
    b. ilegible
    c. ineligible
    d. ileggible

12. It's nobody's _____ if you want to work 10 hours a day.
    a. bussness
    b. busness
    c. bisness
    d. business

13. Though he was late for work, he did not want to appear _____.
    a. inhospitable
    b. unhospital
    c. inhospittable
    d. inhospitible

14. The scientists had found that _____ viruses caused the illness.
    a. muttant
    b. mutent
    c. mutant
    d. myutant

15. She had many _____ works available in her office.
    a. refference
    b. referrance
    c. referance
    d. reference

PART III: LANGUAGE MECHANICS

Choose the answer that shows the best punctuation for the underlined part of sentences 16–20.

16. Did you see an article in the *Chief-Leader* <u>about an upcoming test for the Police department exam.</u>
    a. about an upcoming test for the Police Department exam.
    b. about an upcoming test for the police department exam.
    c. about an upcoming test for the Police department exam?
    d. about an upcoming test for the police department exam?
    e. correct as it is

17. <u>Its a shame that professor Smith</u> never achieved tenure at the university.
    a. Its a shame that Professor Smith
    b. It's a shame that professor Smith
    c. Its a shame, that Professor Smith
    d. It's a shame that Professor Smith
    e. Correct as it is

18. "<u>Look out theres a tornado coming</u>" said the weather expert.
    a. "Look out! There's a tornado coming"
    b. "Look out. Theres a tornado coming."
    c. "Look out! Theres a tornado coming!"
    d. "Look out! There's a tornado coming,"
    e. Correct as it is

19. <u>Though I had to go to work early,</u> I stayed up long past bedtime.
    a. Though I had to go to work early
    b. Though I had to go to work early:
    c. Though I had to go to work early—
    d. Though, I had to go to work early
    e. Correct as it is

20. <u>Its to late to hand in</u> the assignment now.

    a. It's to late to hand in

    b. It's too late too hand in

    c. Its too late to hand in

    d. It's too late to hand in

    e. Correct as it is

PART IV: LANGUAGE EXPRESSION

Choose the word or phrase that best completes each sentence below.

21. They went to _____ house to pick up a change of clothes.

    a. their

    b. they're

    c. there

    d. they

22. She had collected a large _____ of awards in her long career.

    a. number

    b. amount

    c. type

    d. kind

23. The police cruiser responded to an incident that _____ at the corner of Third and Main Streets.

    a. is breaking out

    b. had broke out

    c. was broke out

    d. had broken out

24. There are _____ murders in New York City
this year than last year.
  a. less
  b. fewer
  c. smaller
  d. larger

25. The woman _____ made the quilt was an experienced seamstress.
  a. that
  b. whom
  c. who
  d. which

PART V: MATH

26. 400
  x 76
  a. 52,000
  b. 30,100
  c. 20,400
  d. 3,040
  e. None of these

27. 52,834 ÷ 9 =
  a. 5,870 R4
  b. 5,826 R2
  c. 5,826
  d. 5,871
  e. None of these

28. $4\frac{1}{5}$
$1\frac{2}{5}$
$+\,3\frac{3}{10}$

   a. $9\frac{1}{10}$

   b. $8\frac{9}{10}$

   c. $8\frac{4}{5}$

   d. $8\frac{6}{15}$

   e. None of these

29. $\frac{1}{6} + \frac{7}{12} + \frac{2}{3} =$

   a. $\frac{10}{24}$

   b. $2\frac{1}{6}$

   c. $1\frac{5}{6}$

   d. $1\frac{5}{12}$

   e. None of these

30. $426 - 7.2 =$

   a. 354.0

   b. 425.28

   c. 418.8

   d. 41.88

   e. None of these

31. Which is another way to write $\frac{4}{25}$?

   a. 4%

   b. 16%

   c. 40%

   d. 100%

32. A piece of ribbon 3 feet 4 inches long was divided in 5 equal parts. How long was each part?

   a. 1 foot 2 inches

   b. 10 inches

   c. 8 inches

   d. 6 inches

33. A snack machine accepts only quarters. Candy bars cost 25¢, packages of peanuts cost 75¢, and cans of cola cost 50¢. How many quarters are needed to buy two candy bars, one package of peanuts, and one can of cola?

a. 5

b. 6

c. 7

d. 8

34. The perimeter of a rectangle is 148 feet. Its two longest sides add up to 86 feet. What is the length of each of its two shortest sides?

a. 31 ft.

b. 42 ft.

c. 62 ft.

d. 74 ft.

PART VI: READING COMPREHENSION

Read the paragraphs below and answer the questions that follow.

Since the mid–1980s, there has been considerable controversy over whether college curriculums should continue to offer the so-called core curriculum. Primarily, the core courses consisted of mandatory classes in western history and culture and were intended to form a common foundation of learning for the education of all students. The literature of these courses is commonly referred to as the literary canon. However, college campuses became more ethnically diverse as a result of open enrollments and affirmative action initiatives in the late '60s and '70s. As a result, there were increased demands for college programs to reflect that diversity by the inclusion of programs in ethnic studies and by the abandonment of many literary works that had previously comprised the canon. Feminists, too, called for more study of the works of women authors and accused colleges of limiting their study to the writings of Dead White European Males or DWEMs. Ironically, the call for the end of the canon came just as core courses were being reinstated on many campuses after years of being discarded in favor of programs that were seen as more relevant to modern life. This movement back to the core was largely in response to critics, such as E. D. Hirsch and Alan Bloom, who believe that a shared body of knowledge that is represented by the works in the traditional literary canon is necessary to provide a shared cultural literacy for educated people.

35. The main idea of this paragraph is
   a. colleges should abandon the core curriculum
   b. core courses exclude women
   c. colleges are examining the role of core courses in their curriculums
   d. core courses are open only to European men

36. In this paragraph, the word *mandatory* most nearly means
   a. outdated
   b. optional
   c. required
   d. difficult

37. Bloom and Hirsch believe that the core curriculum
   a. should be eliminated
   b. should be optional
   c. should be required
   d. should be more inclusive

38. The author suggests in this paragraph that
   a. works by DWEMs should be eliminated from the core
   b. the traditional literary canon is outdated
   c. colleges should be more inclusive
   d. works by DWEMs are seen as irrelevant to the experience of women and minorities

Considerable national attention has focused in recent years on the failure of city, state, and national agencies to protect the lives and welfare of children. The public outrage that followed high-profile child abuse cases has meant that more and more children are being taken into foster care to protect them from endangerment in their own homes. This has meant that already overburdened caseworkers are given even larger work loads as they try to cope with the flood of children remanded into care by the courts. In several large cities where the numbers of children threaten to overwhelm the systems designated to provide care, a number of reforms have been instituted to assist them. Among the most promising is the effort to site services in communities rather than at distant social service agencies. Wherever possible, children are being placed with relatives or with foster families in their home communities. They are thus not removed from the neighborhood, extended family, and school connections that serve them well. Case loads have been reduced for many social service workers, and workers are being recruited from the communities that have the greatest need. Social service agencies are insisting upon a uniform data base regarding foster care cases that can be accessed by all those charged with the supervision of children in care. In this way, fewer children can fall through bureaucratic cracks when files are lost or children are moved from one location to another. Sibling groups, too, are kept together as often as possible so that children can maintain family relationships while in foster care.

39. The best title for this paragraph would be
   a. The High Cost of Child Abuse
   b. Child Abuse: A National Scandal
   c. Community-Based Social Work: Helping the Foster System Work
   d. The Risks and Benefits of Foster Care

40. In this paragraph, the word *siblings* refers to
   a. extended family
   b. community groups
   c. foster parents
   d. brothers and sisters

41. Computer access to records is important to social workers so that they can
   a. learn about a child's medical history
   b. keep track of progress on a child's case
   c. keep personal information out of the hands of other social workers
   d. improve computer skills

42. In this paragraph, the author suggests that
   a. in the past, social workers were given little assistance
   b. social workers are lazy
   c. social workers need to take more responsibility
   d. community connections are important to good social work

A narrow fellow in the grass
Occasionally rides;
You may have met him—did you not?
His notice sudden is.

The grass divides as with a comb,
A spotted shaft is seen,
And then it closes at your feet
And opens further on.

He likes a boggy acre,
A floor too cool for corn,
Yet when a boy, and barefoot,
I more than once at noon

Have passed, I thought, a whip-lash
Unbraiding in the sun,
When, stooping to secure it,
It wrinkled, and was gone.

Several of nature's people
I know and they know me;
I feel for them a transport
Of cordiality;

But never met this fellow,
Attended or alone,
Without a tighter breathing
And zero at the bone.

43. Who or what is the *fellow* in this poem?

   a. a whip-lash

   b. a weed

   c. a snake

   d. a gust of wind

44. The phrase "Without a tighter breathing / And zero at the bone" most nearly means

   a. without being frightened

   b. without counting steps

   c. without wearing shoes

   d. without running away

45. The phrase *nature's people* means

   a. campers

   b. environmentalists

   c. animals

   d. vegetarians

46. This poem is most likely set in

   a. Massachusetts

   b. winter

   c. autumn

   d. summer

47. The speaker of this poem is most likely

   a. an adult woman

   b. an adult man

   c. a young girl

   d. a zoo keeper

In the 1990s, when African-American athletes compete in and often dominate nearly every competitive sport, it is difficult to realize that a mere 50 years ago the appearance of a single Black man on a baseball team was a revolutionary event. When Jackie Robinson joined the Brooklyn Dodgers in 1947, he was the first man of his race to play in the major leagues in this country. Though the all-Black Negro Leagues had nourished talented players for years, none had been allowed to play on a team with a national following. After World War II the gradual but persistent initiatives by many Black people to gain their civil rights in their native land meant that it was only a matter of time before our national pastime would be challenged to include players of color. Recruited by Branch Rickey, the general manager of the Dodgers, Jackie Robinson, former football star at the University of California at Los Angeles, finally donned the Dodger uniform. In the beginning, Robinson had to withstand the hostility of some fans and fellow players and was subjected to their insulting and often dangerous behavior. He met insult with dignity, however, and went on to lead his team to six National League pennants and a triumphant defeat of the Yankees in the World Series of 1955. He was elected to the Baseball Hall of Fame in 1962. Despite the pioneering efforts of Rickey, Robinson, and others, it still took many years before all teams were integrated. However, it was their courage and tenacity that allowed baseball to lead other sports to open their ranks to Black athletes and to change the face of American games forever.

48. Which of the following best describes the subject of this passage?
  a. the life of Jackie Robinson
  b. racial discrimination in baseball
  c. Robinson's role in integrating baseball
  d. insulting behavior at baseball games

49. In this paragraph, the word *pioneering* most nearly means
  a. dangerous
  b. refreshing
  c. triumphant
  d. unprecedented

50. When Robinson first played with the Dodgers,
  a. he was welcomed as a hero
  b. he was paid less than other players
  c. he was subjected to insults and threats
  d. he defied the orders of Branch Rickey

Check your answers on this practice test with the *Standardized Test Answers and Explanations* that follow. Note what questions you missed. Plan to spend some time reviewing those areas in which your performance was weak.

STANDARDIZED TEST ANSWERS AND EXPLANATIONS

Part I: Vocabulary

1. b. *Gregarious* means *sociable.*

2. c. *Obsolete* means *outdated.*

3. a. *Innocuous* means *harmless.*

4. a. The opposite of *antipathy* (*dislike*) is *friendship.*

5. d. The opposite of *arrogant* is *humble.*

6. b. The opposite of *impulsive* is *cautious.*

7. b. Food would be a *tantalizing* (*tempting*) smell to someone who hasn't eaten.

8. b. *Pseudonym* means *false name.*

9. d. Only the *benefactor* could have been anonymous. All the others had to be known to the family.

10. b. Because the girl is successful, her blindness is not a *hindrance*, or drawback.

Part II: Spelling

11. a. *Illegible*

12. d. *Business*

13. a. *Inhospitable*

14. c. *Mutant*

15. d. *Reference*

Part III: Language Mechanics

16. d. A question needs a question mark.

17. d. The contraction *it's* needs an apostrophe; Professor Smith is a title and requires a capital letter.

18. d. The contraction *there's* needs an apostrophe; there is a comma after the quotation.

19. e. A comma should come before a clause that begins a sentence.

20. d. The contraction *it's* needs an apostrophe; the sentence requires the adverb *too.*

Part IV: Language Expression

21. a. A possessive pronoun is needed.

22. a. Awards can be counted, so the correct word is *number*.

23. d. *Had broken out* matches the verb *responded*.

24. b. Murders can be counted, so the word needed is *fewer*.

25. c. Use the word *who* when referring to people as subjects.

Part V: Math

26. e. The correct answer is 30,400.

27. a. If you got a different answer, you probably simply made an error in multiplication or subtraction.

28. b. Incorrect answers include adding both the numerator and the denominator and not converting fifths to tenths properly.

29. d. You have to convert all three fractions to twelfths before adding them.

30. c. The other answers were subtracted without aligning the decimal points.

31. b. Four divided by 25 equals 0.16 or 16%.

32. c. Three feet 4 inches equals 40 inches; 40 divided by 5 is 8.

33. c. Two candy bars require 2 quarters; one package of peanuts requires 3 quarters; one can of cola requires 2 quarters—for a total of 7 quarters.

34. a. The first step in solving the problem is to subtract 86 from 148. The remainder, 62, is then divided by 2.

Part VI: Reading Comprehension

35. c. The main idea is the debate over the canon, which means that colleges must examine their own attitudes about the core curriculum.

36. c. The meaning of *mandatory* as *required* is signaled by the reference to the core as being the "common foundation of learning for the education of all students."

37. c. The clue to this answer lies in the sentence that says that Bloom and Hirsch believe that the canon is "necessary to provide a shared cultural literacy for educated people."

38. d. This is implied by the reference to objections both by minorities and by women to the core curriculum.

39. c. The main idea of the passage is that community-based services are needed to help with the rising numbers of children in foster care.

40. d. Siblings are brothers and sisters. The clue here is in the reference to family relationships.

41. b. This detail is in the reference to files being lost and children changing locations while in foster care.

42. d. It is implied throughout the passage that community resources are important to the efficient delivery of child welfare services.

43. c. The *fellow* frightens the speaker, according to the last stanza. In the fourth stanza, the speaker describes seeing something that looks like a whip-lash but then moves away. A snake is the only one of the four choices that could fit these criteria.

44. a. *Tighter breathing* indicates fear, as does *zero at the bone,* since one is sometimes said to be *cold with fear.*

45. c. There are no campers, environmentalists, or vegetarians in the poem.

46. d. The grass in the first two stanzas, the sun in the fourth stanza, and the speaker's bare feet in the third stanza suggest summertime.

47. b. The third stanza contains the phrase *when a boy,* implying that the speaker was a boy in the past and is now, therefore, an adult man.

48. c. This is the most general statement and is therefore the best statement of the subject.

49. d. *Pioneering* implies something that had not been experienced before; therefore, *unprecedented* makes the most sense here.

50. c. This detail is revealed in the sentence " . . . had to withstand the hostility of some fans and fellow players and was subjected to their insulting and often dangerous behavior."

HOW WELL DID I DO ON THE PRACTICE STANDARDIZED TEST? A SELF ANALYSIS

I answered ____/10 questions correctly in the *Vocabulary* section.

I answered ____/5 questions correctly in the *Spelling* section.

I answered ____/5 questions correctly in the *Language Mechanics* section.

I answered ____/5 questions correctly in the *Language Expression* section.

I answered ____/9 questions correctly in the *Math* section.

I answered ____/16 questions correctly in the *Reading Comprehension* section.

I answered the most questions correctly in the

_____ section(s).

I think I did well in these sections because

I did not do as well in the _____

section(s).

I think I did not do as well in these areas because

In order to improve my performance in these sections, I need to

_____ review my basic skills (spelling, vocabulary, math, or grammar)

_____ read questions more carefully

_____ select answers more carefully

_____ work more quickly

_____ work more slowly

Other_____

_____

CHAPTER | 19

In this chapter, you will apply the test-taking strategies you've learned in this book to a sample exam like the one you might find in a college classroom.

TEST YOURSELF: A PRACTICE CLASSROOM TEST

The exam that follows is based on what you have read in this book. It is, therefore, similar to many classroom tests that are based on textbook material.

Like the tests in Chapters 17 and 18, this sample test is longer than 20 minutes; it's designed to take 50 minutes. Your best bet is to vary the 20-minutes-a-day formula and take the full 50 minutes, so you can complete the test in one sitting. Be sure to preview the test and plan your time before you start!

PART I: IDENTIFICATIONS (10 POINTS)

Define or give examples of each of the following.

1. standardized test

_____

2. stems (in testing)

_____

3. mnemonics

_____

4. distributed practice

_____

5. graphic aids

_____

PART II: TRUE/FALSE (10 POINTS)

Mark ten of the following statements as true or false.

_____ **6.** *Connotation* refers to the dictionary definition of a word.

_____ **7.** The GED is an example of a civil service test.

_____ **8.** Distributed practice is best accomplished by cramming.

_____ **9.** A monthly calendar is generally more useful than a weekly calendar in scheduling study time.

_____ **10.** A study group should not have fewer than ten members.

_____ **11.** It is usually not a good idea to study in bed.

_____ **12.** You should spend the same amount of time planning your answer on an essay test as you spend writing the answer.

_____ **13.** *Visualization* refers to a learning modality.

_____ **14.** Procrastination is a method for curing test anxiety.

_____ **15.** It is usually better to use active voice in writing.

_____ **16.** The thesis statement is a review of all the facts in a paragraph.

_____ **17.** You should never play the radio while you are studying.

PART III: MULTIPLE-CHOICE (10 POINTS)

Circle the correct answer in each of the following.

18. All of the following are true of adult test takers EXCEPT
 a. they have a larger store of prior knowledge
 b. they have higher IQs than younger test takers
 c. they have been tested by life experience
 d. they have the maturity that allows them to be more organized learners

19. Instructors favor multiple-choice tests because
 a. they penalize those who have poor language skills
 b. they are more time-consuming to write
 c. they are more difficult
 d. they allow testing of a wider range of skills

20. When you look at the test for the first time you should
 a. start working as soon as possible
 b. do all of the essays first
 c. listen carefully to the instructions
 d. make sure you have pens and pencils

21. Note cards are preferable to notebook pages because
 a. they can contain more information
 b. they are shorter
 c. they are neater
 d. they can be carried in your pocket or purse

22. Judgment questions on civil service tests are concerned with all of the following except
 a. issues of safety
 b. issues of public relations
 c. compliance with regulations
 d. legal aspects of civil service jobs

23. Some multiple-choice questions include questions based on graphic material because
    a. graphics summarize large amounts of information in a small space
    b. graphics are easier to write
    c. graphics are more familiar to adults than to younger learners
    d. graphic questions test listening skills

24. The way to prevent the onset of test anxiety is to
    a. study at least three hours per day
    b. pay attention to small problems
    c. postpone a vigorous diet and exercise plan
    d. keep a well-organized routine and a positive attitude

25. A good place to locate information about civil service tests and test dates is
    a. the Yellow Pages of the telephone book
    b. the public library
    c. the classified ads in the newspapers
    d. a course outline or syllabus

26. When studying before sleep, it is a good idea to
    a. allow at least 30 minutes between study and sleep
    b. watch television to relax between study and sleep
    c. allow no activity or interference between study and sleep
    d. listen to the radio, but do not watch television between study and sleep

27. A monthly calendar is preferable to a weekly calendar in organizing study time because
    a. it is more pleasing to the eye
    b. it can hold more information
    c. it can show clusters of exam activity more easily
    d. it is smaller and easier to handle

PART IV: COMPLETIONS (20 POINTS)

Complete the following sentences.

28. The word that refers to associated word meanings is _____.

29. Incorrect answers on multiple-choice tests are called _____.

30. A test for public employment is called a _____.

31. The process by which tests are analyzed to assess priorities is called _____.

32. Intensive review of selected items immediately prior to a test is called _____.

PART V: EXTENDED-ANSWER QUESTIONS (20 POINTS)

Answer two of the following.

33. Summarize the pros and cons of working with a study group.

34. List three primary learning modalities and give an example of how to work with each.

35. Enumerate the ways to cope with a panic attack during a test.

PART VI: ESSAYS (30 POINTS)

Answer two of the following.

36. Discuss in detail the criteria for writing good answers to essay questions.

37. Describe the causes, effects, and treatments for test anxiety.

38. Compare the advantages and disadvantages of adult and younger test takers.

Check your answers in the *Classroom Test Answers and Explanations* that follow. Grade your test. If your score is disappointing, look back in the book to locate the information you didn't know on the sample test. Then you'll know even more.

CLASSROOM TEST ANSWERS AND EXPLANATIONS

Part I: Identifications

1. a test on which a person's performance is judged in comparison to the performance of many others who took the same test
2. the part of the question that carries the information on which the question is based
3. memory tricks
4. learning in short segments over time
5. maps, charts, diagrams, or illustration that show large amounts of information visually

Part II: True/False

6. **F.** *Connotation* is the associated meaning of a word.
7. **F.** The GED is a standardized test.
8. **F.** Distributed practice is intermittent and can't be used for cramming.
9. **T.** Monthly calendars show more time at a glance.
10. **F.** A study group should have no more than six members.
11. **T.** You might fall asleep if you study in bed.
12. **T.** Half of your time should be spent planning and half writing.
13. **F.** Visualization is a relaxation technique.
14. **F.** Procrastination will only increase anxiety as the test taker delays his work.
15. **T.** Active voice is more powerful than passive voice.
16. **F.** A thesis statement is a preview of the main ideas of an essay.
17. **F.** Beware the absolute. *Never* is too strong a word.

Part III: Multiple-Choice

18. b. IQs have nothing to do with test taking.

19. d. All of the other choices are negative. This is the only one that suggests a reason for favoring this question type.

20. c. If you don't listen to the instructions you may miss valuable information from the instructor.

21. d. The big advantage of note cards is that they are portable.

22. d. Judgment calls don't usually involve legal matters.

23. a. The major virtue of graphic aids is the fact that they pack a lot of information in a very small space.

24. d. Everything else will be easier if you are well-organized.

25. b. The public library contains a wealth of information about many community events, including test dates.

26. c. Any kind of interference gets in the way of remembering what you are studying.

27. c. The layout of a monthly calendar allows for a broader view of a period of time.

Part IV: Completions

28. Associated word meanings are *connotations.*

29. Incorrect answers on multiple-choice tests are called *distractors.*

30. A test for public employment is a *civil service test.*

31. The process by which test questions are analyzed to assess priorities is called *triage.*

32. Intensive review of selected items immediately before a test is called *cramming.*

Part V: Extended Answer Questions

33. Good reasons for a study group:

    a. Benefit of other peoples' ideas

    b. Sharing the work load

    c. Listening and talking to other students helps you remember

Drawbacks to study groups:

    a. Some members don't do the work

    b. Some people socialize more than work

    c. Some competitive people may not share their work

34. Auditory learners learn by listening. They should say out loud what they are learning.

Visual learners learn by seeing. They should color-code important information or map long ideas because they are easier to remember that way.

Kinesthetic learners learn by doing. They should take lots of notes, underline, and make margin notes while reading.

35. Coping with a panic attack during a test:
  a. Put down your pen
  b. Close your eyes
  c. Relax completely
  d. Breathe deeply
  e. Visualize the end of the test
  f. Make yourself more comfortable

Part VI: Essays

36. There are four main guidelines for writing essay answers on tests. Essay answers should be clear, concise, well-organized, and accurate.

In order to be clear on an essay, you should be familiar with the vocabulary of the topic on which you are writing. You should be aware of words that are easily confused, such as *advise* and *advice, affect* and *effect,* for example. You should choose words carefully and be sure that they mean what you want them to mean.

You can be concise in your writing by keeping your sentence structure simple. You should use active voice whenever possible, and use verbs that are very specific to the sentence. Keep the language simple, and don't try to use extra words and phrases that repeat or pad the sentences.

You can organize your essay answers by mapping or outlining the information quickly in the margins or on the back of the essay book. Be sure you start your essay with a good thesis statement, and start each paragraph with a topic sentence.

Your essay answers can be accurate if you pay attention to basic grammar and spelling rules. Make sure your sentences have the proper punctuation. Avoid the mistakes that take away from the content of your essay. These would include using *suppose to* instead of *supposed to* and using an apostrophe to make a plural. For example, "We had nice peach's today."

If you make a mnemonic like COCA (clear, organized, concise, accurate), it may help you to remember the steps to writing a good essay.

37. Test anxiety comes from several sources and is different for each student. The effects of test anxiety can be simple or severe. Fortunately, there are ways of managing and sometimes curing test anxiety for most people.

The reason that some people suffer from test anxiety is that there are both real and imagined risks that they face when taking a big test. Real risks include losing a job, failing to get into a school or job program, or failing a course. In addition, we often imagine risks such as disappointing ourselves and others, facing an uncertain future, or repeating a previous failure.

For many people test anxiety is mild and goes away once the test begins. For others, the effect of test anxiety is nervousness, sleeplessness, and fear of freezing up when they see the test. For some test takers, a little anxiety is good because it energizes them and makes them focus on performing successfully.

The treatments for test anxiety include confronting your fears openly, so you can deal with them. Sometimes this means writing down the problem and then writing down a solution, so you can see it in front of you and feel in control. A second treatment for test anxiety is over-learning, which means to study in such a way that the answers to questions are almost automatic. You should not make excuses for your performance on a test. This makes you a victim and takes away your power over the test. You should also avoid procrastination in studying for your test. Don't hide behind defense mechanisms like rationalizing reasons for failure. And finally, you should visualize success on the test, and let that vision soften the effects of test anxiety.

38. For the test taker, age is not particularly important when it comes to studying for big tests. There are benefits and drawbacks both for adult test takers and for young people who must prepare for important tests.

Adults have some advantages as test takers. They have lived longer and have more experiences on which to draw. They have been tested outside of school in ways that have not been graded but that were important to their lives. Adults have the maturity that enables them to put tests into a proper perspective, cope with test anxiety, and organize their time efficiently.

There are a couple of drawbacks to being an adult test taker, however. Tests for adults may be more serious because they are related to job improvement or job performance that could have long-term consequences. Adults are also likely to be more self-critical and be more self-conscious about their test performance.

Younger test takers have the advantage that they take tests all the time and are used to having tests be part of their daily lives. Often young people have the advantage of being in school full time and thus of being part of the information networks of the school, including access to instructors for questions and support.

The disadvantages for younger test takers include having a shorter attention span, which means that they may not read and follow directions as well as adults who may listen more carefully. They are less likely to organize their time to best advantage and thus be put at risk for cramming at the last minute. They may also lack the emotional maturity to cope with the pressure of a big test.

HOW WELL DID I DO ON THE PRACTICE CLASSROOM TEST? A SELF ANALYSIS

I answered ___/5 questions correctly on the *Identifications* section.

I answered ___/12 questions correctly on the *True/False* section.

I answered ___/10 questions correctly on the *Multiple Choice* section.

If I were the instructor, I would give ___/20 points for the *Extended Answer* responses.

If I were the instructor, I would give ___/30 points for the *Essay* answers.

I performed best on the _____
  section(s) of the test.

I believe I did well on these sections because

I did not perform as well on the _____
  section(s) of the test.

I believe I did not do as well on these sections because

To improve my performance on these sections, I need to
  _____ study more specific information (facts, terms, vocabulary)
  _____ study more general information (concepts, important main ideas)
  _____ organize my answers more efficiently
  _____ review spelling, usage, and punctuation rules

Other_____

_____

CHAPTER 20

You've learned a lot about how to take a test. Now it's time to assess how much you have learned about yourself and analyze the ways you'll work toward even further improving your test-taking skills.

SUMMING UP

Right before the introduction, you took a test survey called "How Can I Get Smarter than the Tests I Take?" Here are some quick answers for your review.

Multiple choice

Why are so many tests made in this format?

They are easier to grade and don't penalize poor writing or language skills.

How do I choose between two answers when they both seem right?

Try turning both answers into True/False questions.

Which should I read first, the questions or the answers?
If the question or stem is long, read the answers or options first.

How do I handle choices like "All of the above" or "None of the above"?
Read the stems carefully to note important terms, and always be wary of questions that are written as absolutes.

True/False

The statements always seem true to me. How do I know when a "true" answer is really false?
Note key words in the question very carefully. Make sure the statement is true in all circumstances.

Sometimes part of the question seems true and another part seems false. How do I know which one to choose?
A true answer must be true in all of its parts.

Matching columns

Why do instructors sometimes put more answers than questions on a matching column?
So you can't use process of elimination in determining an answer.

When two answers are very similar, how do I know which one to choose?
Answer all obvious choices first. Narrow your number of options.

IDs, Fill-ins, or Completions

How much information is required? I never know how much to say.
Put only the information that is required by the question. Don't take up valuable time padding an answer just to show off what you know.

What do I do if I know the answer but have forgotten the spelling?
Spell the word phonetically and hope that the instructor knows the word you mean.

What do I do if I only remember part of an answer?
Put down what you remember. You may get partial credit.

Essay questions
Why are essay questions so popular?
Essays allow students to display a range of skills and knowledge.

How do I make sure I don't run out of time when I write an essay answer?
Make a time frame before you begin to write. Map or diagram your answer before you begin writing.

How do I figure out what to study before an essay test?
Rely on complete class notes, a thorough reading of all assignments, and special attention to points the instructor emphasized throughout the course.

In general
When—and how—should I guess on a test?
When there is no penalty and when you have eliminated all but two possible answers.

How much time should I spend preparing for an exam?
This depends on how important the test is for your personal purposes, how much you already know, and your level of test anxiety.

If I have to cram for a test, how do I do it?
Limit the number of topics you study, make portable notes you can carry with you for odd moments of study, and use multisensory means—seeing, hearing, and writing, for example—to learn the information faster.

Should I study with other people?
If you can study with well-disciplined friends or classmates in an organized and serious way, a study group can be helpful.

In the introduction, you were given a list of statements and asked to check off those that describe your test-taking abilities. Go back to that original list and take a look at those statements again, particularly those you checked off. What have you learned about yourself and about your test-taking skills since you began this book?

Let's find out. That list is repeated below. Read it again and find those statements that you checked off as true. Then respond to the comments accompanying those statements below. Look how far you have come!

1. *I am always nervous about tests.*

   Why do people get nervous on tests?

   In this book, what term is used for nervousness that's related to test taking?

   What can you do to cope with nervousness on tests?

2. *I am nervous on tests only when I don't feel confident about my performance.*

   What can you do to gain the confidence you need to do well on a test?

3. *Sometimes the more I study, the worse I do on exams.*

   Why does this happen?

   How can you get more from your study hours?

4. *If I have time to study, I score better.*

   What are some things you can do to manage time more efficiently?

5. *I do best on tests when I cram for them.*

What are the limits of cramming?

What are some strategies for cramming successfully if you must cram?

6. *When I take a test, I want to know the results immediately.*

Why is it important to you to get the results immediately?

7. *When I take a test, I don't want to know the results immediately.*

Why do you think you want to avoid seeing the test results?

8. *When I get nervous on tests, I freeze up.*

If you panic while you're taking a test, what are some things you can do to overcome your fear?

9. *I do better on essay questions than on short-answer questions.*

Why do you feel more comfortable with essay tests?

10. *I do better on short-answer questions than on essay questions.*

Why are short-answer tests easier for you?

11. *I do better on tests when I study alone.*

Why do you feel better when you study alone?

12. *I do better on tests when I study with a friend.*

How does working with someone else help you to study?

13. *I study better when I am in a quiet room.*

Why is it usually better to study in a quiet room than in a room with the radio or television playing?

14. *I study better when I play the radio or the television.*

What kind of studying can you do effectively when there is background noise in the room?

15. *Sometimes I am surprised when I get a lower score than I expected.*

How can you learn to be more informed about the tests you take?

16. *Sometimes I am graded unfairly.*

What is the best way to approach teachers about tests or about marks on a test?

17. *I sometimes get a better score on a test than I expected.*

Why are you sometimes surprised when you do well on a test?

18. *I sometimes do better on standardized tests than on classroom tests.*

Why are you more confident on a standardized test than on one that was written by your instructor?

19. *I sometimes do better on classroom tests than on standardized tests.*

How do you prepare differently for classroom tests than other tests?

How are standardized and classroom tests different from each other?

20. *Sometimes I study the wrong things for a test.*

How can you be as sure as possible that you are studying the right things for a test?

List three things you've learned about yourself as a learner and a test taker as a result of reading this book:

_____

_____

_____

KEEPING TABS ON YOUR PROGRESS

This book assumes that you will complete at least 3-5 practice tests in each area you want to review. These might include math, vocabulary, reading comprehension, analogies, problem solving, or spelling. Use the chart below to track your progress through your practice tests. Enter the number of questions you answered correctly in each test or section of a test. Enter the percentage of correct answers. When you have completed all the tests in each category that you intend to do, average your grades on all of the tests. (For examples, see the sample table that follows the blank one.) Finally, rate your performance in each category as

S (satisfactory, no further review needed)
N (need some additional review)
U (need much more review)

Subject	Test 1	Test 2	Test 3	Test 4	Test 5	Average	Rating
	/	/	/	/	/		
	%	%	%	%	%		
	/	/	/	/	/		
	%	%	%	%	%		
	/	/	/	/	/		
	%	%	%	%	%		
	/	/	/	/	/		
	%	%	%	%	%		
	/	/	/	/	/		
	%	%	%	%	%		
	/	/	/	/	/		
	%	%	%	%	%		
	/	/	/	/	/		
	%	%	%	%	%		

Suggestions for taking practice tests:

Follow the time limits set by the test. This will give you a realistic idea of how long it may take you to do the test.

Use the results of the practice tests to determine the specific areas you need to spend more time in review.

Subject	Test 1	Test 2	Test 3	Test 4	Test 5	Average	Rating
English	43/75	58/75	63/75	60/75	68/75	77	N
	57%	77%	84%	80%	90%		
Math	50/60	52/60	54/60	56/60	58/60	90	S
	83%	86%	90%	93%	96%		
Reading	25/40	28/40	32/40	34/40	36/40	77	N
	62%	70%	80%	85%	90%		
Science	18/40	23/40	28/40	30/40	32/40	65	U
	45%	57%	70%	75%	80%		

This table was based on the four sections of the ACT 2000 test.

In Short

If you've been following the 20-minute-a-day format, you've lived with this book for several weeks. You know it well—and you know yourself even better now. The strategies you've learned should help you to prepare for and take any kind of test, from a short-answer quiz in a classroom, to a three-hour standardized test for college entrance.

Keep in mind that as an adult, you have many advantages as a test taker. You have experience and the good judgment of maturity on your side. And you're motivated to do well because you're eager to move ahead—in your life and in your career. The word *motivate* comes from a root word meaning *to move*. Let this book help to move you ahead on the job or in school.

So go for it, and take that test. Success is out there—within your reach!

APPENDIX A
THE ANSWER GRID

Most tests, either paper or electronic, use an answer grid on which answers are entered in "bubbles," small circle or ovals on the test page or screen. Here are some reminders on how to use an answer grid:

As always, read the directions carefully.

Make sure all bubbles are completely filled in.

If you want to change an answer, erase the first choice completely.

Make sure you don't leave extra marks around on the paper.

And here is a suggestion: Some students find it difficult to keep track of which row of bubbles matches the question they are working on. A good way to work with this kind of grid is to mark all of the answers in a short section *in the book* or *on scrap paper,* then transfer them all at once to the answer grid. You are less likely to lose your place on the answer sheet if you are entering a *group* of answers than if you are moving back and forth from test to answer sheet with each question.

1. Ⓐ Ⓑ Ⓒ Ⓓ Ⓔ
2. Ⓐ Ⓑ Ⓒ Ⓓ Ⓔ
3. Ⓐ Ⓑ Ⓒ Ⓓ Ⓔ
4. Ⓐ Ⓑ Ⓒ Ⓓ Ⓔ
5. Ⓐ Ⓑ Ⓒ Ⓓ Ⓔ

APPENDIX B
ADDITIONAL RESOURCES

f you want more help with test-taking, here are some resources you can use.

MEDIA RESOURCES
Study Skills and Strategies

Becoming a Master Student by David Ellis, College Survival, 1997.

Study Skills in Practice by J. Deem, Houghton Mifflin, 1992.

Specific Skill Areas

30 Days to a More Powerful Vocabulary by Norman Funk and Norman Lewis, Pocket Books, 1993.

Practical Math in 20 Minutes a Day by Judith Robinovitz, LearningExpress, 1996.

Read Better, Remember More by Elizabeth Chelsa, LearningExpress, 2 ed. 2000.

Improve Your Writing for Work by Elizabeth Chelsa, LearningExpress, 2 ed, 2000.

Grammar Essentials by Judith F. Olson, LearningExpress, 2 ed, 2000.

A Writer's Reference, by Diana Hacker, St. Martin's Press, 1992.

The Princeton Review Word Smart: How to Build a More Educated Vocabulary (on audio cassette) by John Katzman and Adam Robinson, Crown Audio Cassettes, 1993.

Civil Service Tests

LearningExpress, the publisher of this book, publishes test preparation books for many civil service occupations. See the order information at the back of this book. The books listed there are also available in bookstores and libraries.

ARCO also publishes test preparation books for major civil service tests in skilled trades and in basic skill jobs. The series also includes the *Civil Service Handbook* and *General Test Practice for 101 U.S. Jobs.* They are available at major bookstores and public libraries.

Books About Standardized Tests

Peterson's *ACT Success* (Includes a CD-ROM), Princeton, NJ, 1999.

Barron's *How to Prepare for the SAT 1,* 20th Edition, 1998.

TOEFL Sample Tests, 6th Edition (book and audio tape), ETS; available for paper test and the new computer based test.

Teach Yourself the SAT in 24 Hours, Arco, 1999.

8 Real SATs, College Board, 1996.

The Best Test Preparation for the GED: General Educational Development, Scott Cameron, Research and Education Association, 1992.

ACT-In-A-Week, Kaplan, Simon & Schuster, 1996.

More About Standardized Tests, on Disk

Acing the New SAT CD-ROM: Your One-on-One Personal SAT Tutor, Penguin Electronics, 1995.

Kaplan SAT and PSAT, with CD-ROM, Simon & Schuster, 1997.

Barron's Computer Study Program for the GED: High School Equivalency Examination for Windows and MacIntosh, Barron's, 1996.

Standardized Tests on Television

GED on TV is aired on public broadcasting stations. It is a series of lessons to prepare viewers for taking the GED. For air dates and further information, call your local public television station.

INTERNET RESOURCES

On the Internet, search engines such as Yahoo!, Netscape, and WebMaster can put you in touch with publishers and other sources of information that can help you prepare for and take a variety of tests.

America Online has Barron's Book Notes for reviewing works of literature, guides to the major publishers, and test prep centers. In addition, online tutoring is available through the Internet. Students post questions and teachers answer them online. GED prep courses are also offered through the Internet. Subscribers have the option of taking all five parts or a single course. Fees vary.

The Online Computer Library Center is available at *http://www.oclc.org.*

COMMUNITY RESOURCES

Private Courses

For specific kinds of tests, such as nursing or civil service exams, community experts in the field often teach short-term review courses or seminars. You can find out about such courses in the yellow pages of the phone book, through the departmental office at a local high school or college, or at union headquarters in your city. Fees for these classes are set by the individual practitioner.

Tutoring

Some test takers feel that they need some one-on-one tutoring to prepare them for an important test. This may be true especially if there is a particular skill, like math or writing, that you feel you may be weak in, or that you need to improve with the help of a professional. Tutors advertise in local newspapers, on bulletin boards at schools and libraries, and in the yellow pages of the telephone book. If possible, it is a good idea to get a referral from someone who knows the tutor and his or her reputation in the community. Before hiring a tutor, be sure that you find out about his or her experience and expertise. Find out how long that person has been in the tutoring business. You may find someone who knows the subject well, but does not know how communicate knowledge in a patient and helpful manner. Private tutors are often quite expensive, so you owe it to yourself to interview a prospective tutor the way you would any other employee.

Commercial Exam Prep Courses

Thousands of students, old and young, enroll in the large exam prep courses offered for SAT and other test preparation every year. These courses, such as the Princeton Review and Kaplan, offer tightly organized, programmed materials to assist in the preparation for college and professional examinations. They are taught by enthusiastic, well-educated people who inspire students to do well and to be successful on the tests. Often the classes are supplemented by computer software and interactive learning labs available to customers. Courses such as these have a good reputation.

There are some drawbacks, however. These courses tend to be quite expensive and so are out of the range of many test takers. Like anything else, getting the most—and the most for your money—requires a commitment by the learner to conscientiously use the tapes, study the words, and take the practice quizzes. For some people, the monetary investment makes the motivation! For others, schedule conflicts and other problems make it difficult to take full advantage of the program; they may have wasted money that could have gone to hiring a tutor or taking another kind of course.

Achieve Test Success
With LearningExpress

Our acclaimed series of academic and other job related exam guides are the most sought after resources of their kind. Get the edge with the only exam guides to offer the features that test-takers have come to expect from LearningExpress—The Exclusive LearningExpress Advantage:

- **THREE** Complete practice tests based on official exams
- Vital review of skills tested and hundreds of sample questions with full answers and explanations
- The exclusive LearningExpress Test Preparation System—must know exam information, test-taking strategies, customized study planners, tips on physical and mental preparation and more.

Easy to Use & Understand

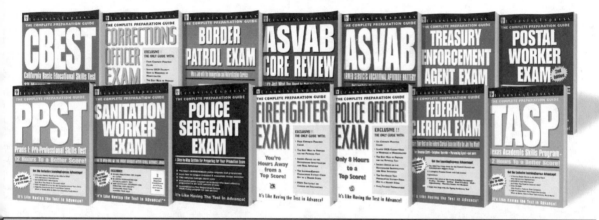

Also available at your local bookstore. Prices Subject to Change Without Notice.

LEARNINGEXPRESS®

LearnATest.com™

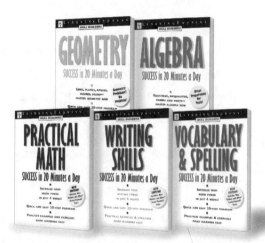